MW01290902

Bestselling books by Heather Baker

Speed Writing
Modern Shorthand
ISBN: 978-1532704918

How to Take Minutes
of Meetings
ISBN: 978-1532737602

Successful Business
Writing
ISBN: 978-1532737688

Bestselling books from UoLearn

How to Write
Excellent Reports
ISBN: 978-1849370899

Developing Your
Assertiveness
ISBN: 978-1537637723

Developing Your
Influencing Skills
ISBN: 978-1537637785

Order books from Amazon or your favorite
bookseller and from www.uolearn.com

Speed Writing Dictionary
Over 7700 Words
An Alternative to Shorthand

Speedwriting dictionary from the BakerWrite system a modern alternative to shorthand including all the 4000 most common words in English. US/international spelling edition.

Published by: Universe of Learning Ltd, reg number 6485477, Lancashire, UK, www.UoLearn.com, support@UoLearn.com

Copyright © 2016
by Joanna Gutmann, Heather Baker and Margaret Greenhall

The moral right of these authors has been asserted.

First Published 2016

ISBN: 978-1534683204

All rights reserved. No part of this book may be reproduced either electronically or on paper without permission in writing from the publisher, except for passages of less than 500 words for purposes of review.

Universe of Learning and UoLearn are trademarks of Universe of Learning Ltd.
BakerWrite is a trademark of Baker Thompson Associates Ltd and is used with permission.

Edited by Dr Margaret Greenhall.

The publisher and author assume no liability for any loss or damage, personal or otherwise which is directly or indirectly caused by the application of any of the contents of this book.

Speed writing dictionary
US/International spelling edition

This extended dictionary is the work of three authors.
The BakerWrite speed writing system was created by Heather
Baker as an easy to learn alternative to shorthand.
She produced a short dictionary to go along with the course
and Joanna Gutmann, a licensed BakerWrite trainer, expanded
this to several thousand words. Margaret Greenhall then added
to this dictionary and edited it.

This book includes all 4000 of the most common words in
written English and lots of business, educational and medical
terms.

The BakerWrite system is explained in the companion volume
by Heather Baker:

Speed Writing Modern Shorthand
An Easy to Learn Note Taking System,
Heather Baker
ISBN: 978-1532704918
3rd Edition

This is available from Amazon.

This book is intended for you to use interactively.
Please add your own variations as the idea is that it is a
reference unique to you. So please feel free to write in the book,
that's what the lines are for on each page and the spare pages
at the back of the book.
We've worked hard to put in a massive number of words and
if you have any suggestions for extra words please let us know
and we can add them into the next edition.

If you need any help customer support is available via email
support@uolearn.com, weekdays, UK time.

The Authors

Heather Baker

Heather had over twenty years' experience as a secretary and PA before setting up Baker Thompson Associates Limited in 2000. The company specializes in the training and development of PAs and administrative staff, www.bakerthompsonassoc.co.uk.
She is an acclaimed international speaker and has worked in a wide variety of places including London, Liverpool, Paris, Abu Dhabi, Dubai, Singapore, Melbourne, Sydney and Johannesburg. She is a best-selling author of books on speed writing, minute taking and business writing.
Heather worked for ICI Pharmaceuticals (now AstraZeneca) and Hewlett Packard. She spent 5 years in France working for the Commercial Director of Cognac Hine and then 10 years with Granada Media working up to Personal Assistant to the Managing Director, commuting regularly between their offices in Manchester and London.
She created this speed writing system based on some of the principles of shorthand to fulfill a requirement by many companies for a quick and easy way for their employees to take notes. Her speedwriting book is an international best seller.

Joanna Gutmann

Joanna became involved in training whilst working in a PA role in a training center during the development of a major training program in office and customer-focused communication skills. She left to start her business in the early nineties and continued to work in that area, increasingly specializing in business writing , www.joanna-gutmann.co.uk
Some 15 years ago, inquiries about minute taking increased noticeably which led Joanna to research the area in detail. Having taken minutes for years, she developed a one day

programme which gives both the knowledge and the skill to work effectively as a minute taker and that led to her writing the highly successful, 'Taking Minutes of Meetings' (Kogan Page). Today, her business is focused on 'the meeting' with training on chairing, report writing and speed reading

Joanna is delighted to hold a licence to run the BakerWrite speed writing training and has found it an invaluable complement to both minute taking and speed reading training. Joanna is also the author of See Me (Blue Ocean) which helps people present the impression of confidence and competence at work and pocket-sized books on punctuation and professional layout.

Margaret Greenhall

Margaret was a chemistry lecturer for eight years and it was during this time that she was asked to teach the foundation study skills to the new students. This started her interest in how people learn and how the learning environment can help them learn better. She moved to staff development and again learned more about how people share information with each other.

In 2003 Margaret left the university to start a training business, www.inspirachange.co.uk specializing in helping people to understand and share information easily and efficiently. This includes topics such as speed reading, improve your memory, creative problem solving and report writing.

She is the best-selling author of Report Writing Skills, (978-1849370899) and combines face to face training with a portfolio of writing and publishing.

A

a	a
abandon	abndn
abandonment	abndn^m
abate	abt
abdomen	abdmn
abduct	abdct
abduction	abdc^n
aberration	abr^n
abeyance	aby^c
ability	a^{bty}
able	b
abolish	abl$_s$
abolition	abl^n
abomination	abmn^n
abortion	abr^n
about	abt
above	abv
abrasion	abr^n
abroad	abrd
abscond	abscnd
absconded	abscndd
absence	abs^c
absolute	abslt
absolutely	abslt^y
absorb	absrb
absorption	absrp^n
abstinence	abstn^c
abstract	abstrct
abundance	abnd^c
abuse	abus
academia	acdma

academic	acdmc
accelerate	aclrt / acel
accent	acnt
accept	acpt
acceptable	acpt^b
acceptance	acpt^c
access	acs
accessible	acs^b
accident	acdnt
accidental	acdntl
accommodate	^{ac}dt
accommodation	^{ac}dt^n
accompany	^{ac}pny
accomplish	^{ac}pl$_s$
accomplishment	^{ac}pl$_s$^{m}
accord	acrd
according	acrd^g
account	acnt
accountability	acnt^{bty}
accountable	acnt^b
accountant	acntnt
accounting	acnt^g
accrue	acru
accuracy	acrcy
accurate	acrt
accurately	acrt^y
accusation	acus^n
accuse	acus
achievable	a$_c$v^b
achieve	a$_c$v
achieved	a$_c$vd
achievement	a$_c$v^m
acid	acd
acknowledge	aknlj
acknowledged	aknljd

acne	acn	adjacent	ajcnt
acquire	aqir	adjoining	ajn^g
acquisition	aqs^n	adjourn	ajrn
acquit	aqt	adjournment	ajrn^m
acquitted	aqtd	adjust	ajst
across	acrs	adjustable	ajst^b
act	act	adjustment	ajst^m
action	ac^n	administer	admnstr/ +mnstr
activate	actvt		
activation	actv^n	administration	admnstr^n / adm/+mnstr^n
active	actv		
actively	actv^y	administrative	admnstrtv / +mnstrtv
activist	actvst		
activity	actvy	administrator	admnsttr/ +mnsttr
actor	actr		
actress	actrs	admiration	admr^n /+mr^n
actual	actl	admire	admr / +mr
actually	act^y	admissible	adms^b /+ms^b
acute	acut	admission	adm^n / +m^n
ad	+	admit	admt / +mt
adapt	adpt / +pt	admittance	admt^c / +mt^c
adaptable	adpt^b / +pt^b	adolescence	adls^c / +ls^c
adaptation	adpt^n / +pt^n	adolescent	adlsnt / +lsnt
adaption	adp^n / +p^n	adopt	adpt / +pt
add	+ / ad	adoption	adp^n / +p^n
added	+d	adorable	adr^b / +r^b
addict	adct / +ct	adoration	adr^n / +r^n
addiction	adct^n / +ct^n	adore	adr / +r
addition	ad^n / +t^n	adrenal	adnrl / +nrl
additional	ad^{nl} / +t^{nl}	adult	adlt / +lt
address	adrs / +rs	advance	adv^c / +v^c
adept	adpt / +pt	advanced	adv^cd / $\text{+v}^c\text{d}$
adequate	adqt / +qt	advancement	adv^{cm} / +v^{cm}
adequately	adqt^y / +qt^y	advantage	advntg/+vntg
adherence	adhr^c / +hr^c	advantageous	advntgos / +vntags
adhesion	adh^n / +h^n		

advent	advnt / +vnt	again	agn
adventure	advntr /+vntr	against	agnst
adverse	advrs / +vrs	age	ag / aj
advert	advrt / +vrt	agency	ag^{cy}
advertise	advrts / +vrts	agenda	agnda / agn
advertisement	advrts^m/+/ad	agent	agnt
advertising	advrts^g/+vrts^g	aggression	agr^n
advice	advc / +vc	aggressive	agrsv
advisable	advs^b / +vs^b	ago	ago
advise	advs / +vs	agonize	agniz
advised	advsd / +vsd	agony	agny
adviser	advsr / +vsr	agree	agre
advisory	advs^y / +vs^y	agreeable	agre^b
advocate	advct / +vct	agreed	agrd
aesthetic	a$_t$tc	agreement	agr^m
affable	af^b	agricultural	agrcltrl
affair	afr	agriculture	agrcltr / agri
affect	afct	ah	ah
affectation	afct^n	ahead	ahd
affection	afc^n	aid	ad
affiliate	aflit	aide	ad
affiliation	afli^n	AIDS	ads
affirm	afrm	ailment	al^m
affirmation	afrm^n	aim	am
affliction	aflc^n	air	ar
affluence	aflu^c	aircraft	arcrft
afford	afrd	airline	arln
affordability	afrd^{bty}	airplane	arpln / pln
affordable	afrd^b	airport	arprt
afraid	afrd	airway	arwy
African	afrcn	aisle	asl
African-American	afrcn-am	alarm	alrm
after	aftr	album	albm
afternoon	aftrnn / pm	alcohol	alchl
afterward	aftrwrd	alcoholism	alchlsm
		alert	alrt

alien	alin	altogether	altgtr
alienation	alin^n	aluminum	almnm / al
align	alin	always	alws
alignment	alin^m	AM	am
alike	alk	am	am
alive	alv	amass	ams
all	al	amaze	amz
allegation	alg^n	amazement	amz^m
alleged	algd	amazing	amz^g
allegedly	algd^y	ambassador	ambsdr
allegiance	alegi^c	ambiance	amb^c
allergen	alrgn	ambition	amb^n
allergy	alrgy	ambitious	ambtos
alleviate	aleviat	ambulance	ambl^c
alley	aly / a^y	ambush	amb$_s$
alliance	ali^c	amend	amnd
allocate	alct	amended	amndd
allocated	alctd	amendment	amnd^m
allocation	alc^n	American	amrcn / am
allot	alt	amicable	amc^b
allotment	alt^m	amid	amd
allow	alw	among	amng
allowance	alw^c	amount	amnt
allusion	alu^n	amplify	amplfy
ally	aly / a^y	amputate	amptt
almost	almst	amputated	ampttd
alone	aln	amputation	ampt^n
along	alng	amuse	amus
alongside	alngsd	amusement	amus^m
already	alrdy	an	a
also	als	analgesia	anlgsa
alter	altr	analysis	anlyss
alteration	altr^n	analyst	anlyst
altercation	altrc^n	analyze	anlyz
alternative	altrntv	analyzed	anlyzd
although	al$_t$o	anatomy	antmy

ancestor	anstr	anybody	nybdy
ancient	ancnt	anymore	nymr
and	&	anyone	nyon / an1
and/or	&/r	anything	ny_t^g
and so on	etc	anyway	nywy
anemia	anma	anywhere	$ny_w r$
anesthetic	$ans_t tc$	apart	aprt
anesthetist	$ans_t tst$	apartment	$aprt^m$
angel	angl	apologies	aplgs
anger	angr	apologize	aplgiz
angle	angl	apology	ap^o
angry	ang^y	apparent	aprnt
animal	anml	apparently	$aprnt^y$
animation	anm^n	appeal	apel
ankle	ankl	appear	apr
anniversary	$anvrs^y$ / ani	appearance	apr^c
announce	an^c	append	apnd
announcement	an^{cm}	apple	apl
annoy	anoy	appliance	$apli^c$
annoyance	$anoy^c$	applicant	aplcnt
annual	anul	application	$aplc^n$
annually	anu^y	apply	ap^y
annul	anl	appoint	apnt
anonymous	anyms/anom	appointed	apntd
another	$ano_t r$	appointment	$apnt^m$
answer	ansr	apportion	apr^n
answerable	$ansr^b$	appraisal	aprsl
anteater	antetr	appraise	aprs
antelope	antlp	appreciable	$a^p ci^b$
antibiotic	antbotc	appreciate	$a^p cit$
anticipate	antcpt	appreciation	$a^p ci^n$
antismoking	$antsmk^g$	apprehensive	$a^p nsv$
antisocial	$ants^s$	apprentice	$a^p ntc$
anxiety	anxty	approach	a^p_c
anxious	anxs	appropriate	$a^p rt$
any	ny		

approval	a^pvl	arthritis	$a_t$rits
approve	a^pv	article	artcl
approved	a^pvd	articulate	artclt
approximate	aprxmt/aprox	artifact	artfct
approximately	aprxmt^y	artificial	artf^s
	aprox^y	artisan	artsn
April	ap	artist	artst
aptitude	aptd / apt	artistic	artstc
Arab	arb	as	as
arbitration	arbtr^n	ash	a_s
arch	ar$_c$	Asian	asn / a^n
architect	ar$_c$tct	aside	asd
architecture	ar$_c$tctr	ask	ask
archive	ar$_c$v	asleep	aslp
are	r	aspect	aspct
area	ara	Aspergers	asprgrs
arena	arna	ass	as
arguable	argu^b	assault	aslt
argue	argu	assemble	asmbl
argument	argu^m	assembly	asmb^y
arise	aris	assert	asrt
arm	arm	assertion	asr^n
armed	armd	assertive	asrtv
army	army	assess	ass
around	arnd	assessment	ass^m
arrange	arng / arnj	assessor	assr
arrangement	arng^m	asset	ast
array	ary	assign	asin
arrest	arst	assignation	asgn^n
arrival	arvl	assignment	asin^m
arrive	arv	assist	asst
arrogance	arog^c	assistance	asst^c
arrogant	arognt	assistant	astnt
arrow	arw	associate	asocit
art	art	associated	asocitd
artery	art^y	association	asoci^n

assorted	asrtd	audible	aud^b
assortment	asrt^m	audience	audi^c
assume	asum	audio conference	aud^cfr^c
assumption	asmp^n	audit	audt
assurance	asr^c	audition	aud^n
assure	$a_s r$	August	au
assured	$a_s rd$	aunt	ant
astonish	astn_s	authentic	au_tntc
astound	astnd	authenticate	au_tnct
astronomer	astrnmr	author	$\text{au}_t r$
astronomy	astrnmy	authority	au_trty
at	@	authorization	au_trz^n
athlete	$a_t lt$	authorize	au_trz
athletic	$a_t ltc$	autism	autsm
atmosphere	atmsfr/atmos	autistic	autstc
atom	atm	auto	auto
atop	atp	automatic	automtc
attach	at_c	automatically	automtc^y
attachment	$\text{at}_c^{\ m}$	automobile	autombl/auto
attack	atk	autonomy	autonmy
attacked	atkd	availability	avl^{bty}
attain	atn	available	avl^b
attainable	atn^b	average	avrj / ave
attainment	atn^m	aversion	avr^n
attempt	atmpt	avoid	avd
attend	atnd	avoidable	avd^b
attendance	atnd^c	avoidance	avd^c
attendee	atnde	await	awt
attention	atn^n	awake	awk
attitude	atitd	award	awrd
attorney	atrny	aware	awr
attract	atrct	awareness	awrns
attraction	atrc^n	away	awy
attractive	atrcv	awful	aw^f
attribute	atrbt / atrib		
auction	auc^n		

B

baby	bby / bb	bar	br
bachelor	b$_c$lr	bare	br / bar
back	bk	barely	br^y
backdate	bkdt	bargain	brgn
backdated	bkdtd	barn	brn
background	bkgrnd	barrel	brl
backup	bkup	barrier	brr
backyard	bkyrd	barrister	brstr
bacteria	bctra	base	bs
bad	bd	baseball	bsbl
badly	bd^y	basement	bs^m
baffle	bfl	bashful	b$_s$^{f}
bag	bg	basic	bsc
baguette	bget	basically	bsc^y
bake	bk / bak	basis	bss
balance	bl^c	basket	bskt
balanced	bl^{c}d	basketball	bsktbl
ball	bl	bat	bt
balloon	blon	batch	b$_c$
ballot	blt	bath	b$_t$
ban	bn	bathroom	b$_t$rm
banana	bnna	battery	bt^y
band	bnd	battle	btl
banish	bn$_s$	be	b
bank	bnk	beach	b$_c$
banker	bnkr	beam	bm
banking	bnk^g	bean	bn
bankrupt	bnkrpt	bear	br
bankruptcy	bnkrptc	bearable	br^b
bankrupted	bnkrptd	beard	brd
banquet	bnqt	beast	bst
		beat	bt
		beautiful	bti^f
		beauty	bty
		because	bcas

beckon	bkn	benevolent	bnvlnt
become	bcm	bereaved	brevd
bed	bd	bereavement	brev^m
bedroom	bdrm	beside	bsd
bee	be	besides	bsds
beef	bf	bespoke	bspk
been	b	best	bst
beer	br	bet	bt
before	bfr / b4	better	btr
befriend	bfrnd	between	btwn
beg	bg	bewildered	bwldrd
began	bgn	bewildering	bwldr^g
begin	bgn	beyond	bynd
beginning	bgn^g	bias	bs
behalf	bhlf	Bible	b^b
behave	bhv	bicycle	bcycl / bike
behavior	bhvr	bid	bd
behavioral	bhvrl	bidder	bdr
behind	bhnd	big	bg
being	b	bike	bk / bik
belief	blf	bill	bl
believable	blv^b	billion	bln / 10^9
believe	blv	bind	bind / bnd
bell	bl	binge	bng / bnj
belly	b^y	biography	bgrfy / b^o
belong	blng	biological	b^{o}cl
below	blw / blo	biology	b^o
belt	blt	bioscience	biosi^c
bemused	bmsd	birch	br$_c$
bench	bn$_c$	bird	brd
bend	bnd	birth	br$_t$
beneath	bn$_t$	birthday	br$_t$dy
beneficial	bnf^s	bishop	b$_s$p
benefit	bnft	bit	bt
benevolence	bnvl^c	bite	bit
		bitter	btr

black	blk	bomb	bmb
bladder	bldr	bombing	bmb^g
blade	bld	bond	bnd
blame	blm	bone	bn
blank	blnk	bone marrow	bnmrw
blanket	blnkt	bonus	bns
blast	blst	book	bk
blaze	blz	bookkeeper	bkkpr
bleed	bled	bookkeeping	$bkkp^g$
blemish	blm_s	boom	bm / bom
blend	blnd	boost	bst
bless	bls	boot	bt / bot
blessing	bls^g	booth	b_t / bo_t
blind	blnd	border	brdr
blink	blnk	bordered	brdrd
block	blk	bore	br
blog	blg	boring	br^g
blond	blnd	born	brn
blood	bld	borrow	brw
bloody	bldy	boss	bs
blossom	blsm	botany	btny
blotch	bl_c	both	b_t
blow	blw	bother	$b_t r$
blue	blu	bottle	btl
bluff	blf	bottom	btm
blunder	blndr	bought	bt
blur	blr	bounce	bo^c
blurt	blrt	bound	bnd / bond
blush	bl_s	boundary	bnd^y
board	brd	bow	bw / bo
boast	bost	bowel	bwl
boat	bt	bowl	bwl
body	bdy	box	bx
boil	bol	boy	by
bold	bld	boycott	byct
bolt	blt	boyfriend	byfrnd

brain	brn	broke	brk
brake	brk	broken	brkn
branch	brn_c	broker	brkr
brand	brnd	bronze	brnz
brave	brv	brother	br_tr
bread	brd	brought	brt
break	brk	brown	brn
breakable	brk^b	brown field	brnfld
breakdown	brkdn	brush	br_s
breakfast	brkfst	brutal	brtl
breakthrough	brk_tru	brutalized	brtlzd
breast	brst	bubble	bbl
breath	br_t	buck	bk
breathable	br_t^b	bucket	bkt
breathe	br_te	Buddhist	bdst
breathing	br_t^g	buddy	bdy
breeze	brz	budget	bdgt
brick	brk	buffalo	bflo
bricklayer	brklyr	bug	bg
bridal	brdl	build	bld
bride	brd / brid	builder	bldr
bridesmaid	brdsmd	building	bld^g
bridge	brg / brj	bulb	blb
brief	brf	bulk	blk
briefly	brf^y	bull	bl
bright	brt	bullet	blt
brilliance	$brli^c$	bulletin	bltn
brilliant	brlint / bril	bullied	bld
bring	br^g	bully	b^y
bringing	br^{gg}	bunch	bn_c
British	brt_s / brit	bungalow	bnglw
broach	br_c	bungle	bngl
broad	brd	buoyant	bynt
broadcast	brdcst	burden	brdn
brochure	br_sr	bureau	bru
		burn	brn

burning	brn^g		
bury	b^y		
bus	bs		
bush	b$_s$		
business	bsns / bs		
businessman	bsnsmn		
businesswoman	bsnswmn		
busy	bsy		
but	bt		
butcher	bt$_c$r		
butt	bt		
butter	btr		
butterfly	btrf^y		
button	btn		
buy	by / bi		
buyer	byr / bir		
by	by / bi		

C

cab	cb
cabin	cbn
cabinet	cbnt
cable	c^b
cage	cg / cj
cake	ck
calculate	clcult / calc
calculation	clcul^n
calendar	clndr / cal
calibrate	clbrt
calibration	clbr^n
caliper	clpr
call	cl
caller	clr
calm	clm
calories	clrs / cals
came	cm
camera	cmra
camp	cmp
campaign	cmpn
campus	cmps
can't	cnt
can	cn / k
Canadian	cndn / ca
cancel	cncl / kncl
canceled	cncld
cancellation	cncl^n
cancer	cncr / kncr
candidate	cndt
candle	cndl
candy	cndy

Word	Short	Word	Short
canvas	cnvs	cart	crt
canvass	cnvs	cartilage	crtlg / crtlj
cap	cp	cartoon	crtn
capability	cp^{blty}	carve	crv
capable	cp^{b}	carwash	crw_{s}
capacity	cpcty	cascade	cscd
capital	cptl	case	cs
capitalize	cptliz	cash	$c_{s.}$
capped	cpd	cashier	$c_{s}ier$
capsule	cpsul	casino	csno
captain	cptn	cast	cst
caption	cp^{n}	castigated	cstgtd
captivated	cptvtd	castigation	$cstg^{n}$
captivating	$cptvt^{g}$	casual	csul
captive	cptv	casualty	csulty
capture	cptr	cat	ct
car	cr	catalog	ctalg
carbohydrate	crbhydrt/carb	catch	c_{c}
carbon	crbn	catchment	c_{c}^{m}
carbonation	$crbn^{n}$	category	ctg^{y} / cat
card	crd	cater	ctr
cardiac	crdac	caterpillar	ctrplr
cardio	crdio	cathedral	$c_{t}drl$
cardiologist	crdiolgst	catheter	$c_{t}tr$
care	car	Catholic	$c_{t}olc$ / cath
career	crr	cattle	ctl
careful	car^{f}	caught	ct
carefully	car^{fy}	causation	csa^{n}
carer	carr	cause	cs
caretaker	cartkr	causes	css
cargo	crgo	caution	c^{n}
carpenter	crpntr	cave	cv
carpet	crpt	cavity	cvty
carrier	crr	cease	ces
carrot	crt	ceiling	cl^{g}
carry	c^{y}	celebrate	clbrt

celebration	clbr^n	channel	$_c$nl
celebrity	clbrty	chaos	$_c$s / kos
cell	cl / sl	chaplain	$_c$pln
cemetery	cmt^y	chapter	$_c$ptr
censor	cnsr	character	$_c$rctr
censorship	cnsr^p	characteristic	$_c$rctrstc
censure	cnsr	characterize	$_c$rctrz
censured	cnsrd	charge	$_c$rg
cent	cnt	chargeable	$_c$rg^b
center	cntr	charitable	$_c$rt^b
centipede	cntpd	charity	$_c$rty
central	cntrl	charm	$_c$rm
century	cnt^y	chart	$_c$rt
CEO	ceo	charter	$_c$rtr
ceremony	crmny	chartered	$_c$rtrd
certain	crtn	chase	$_c$s
certifiable	crtfi^b	chasten	$_c$sn
certificate	crtfct / cert	chat	$_c$t
certify	crtfy	cheap	$_c$p
cervical	crvcl	cheat	$_c$t
cessation	cs^n	check	$_c$k
chain	$_c$n	cheek	$_c$k / $_c$ek
chainsaw	$_c$nsw	cheer	$_c$r
chair	$_c$r	cheese	$_c$es
chairman	$_c$rmn	chef	$_c$f
chairperson	$_c$rprsn	chemical	$_c$mcl
chairwoman	$_c$rwmn	chemistry	$_c$mst^y / chem
challenge	$_c$lng	chemotherapy	$_c$mo$_t$rpy/chemo
chamber	$_c$mbr	chest	$_c$st
champion	$_c$mpin/champ	chew	$_c$w
championship	$_c$mpin^p	chick	$_c$k
chance	$_c$n^c	chicken	$_c$kn
change	$_c$ng	chief	$_c$f
changeable	$_c$ng^b	child	$_c$ld
changing	$_c$ng^g	childhood	$_c$ldhd

childminder	$_c$ldmndr	civil	cvl
children	$_c$ldrn	civilian	cvln / civi
chill	$_c$l	civilization	cvlza^n
chimpanzee	$_c$mpnz / $_c$mp	civilize	cvlz
chin	$_c$n	claim	clm
Chinese	$_c$ns	clarified	clrfd
chip	$_c$p	clarify	clrfy
chocolate	$_c$clt	clash	cl$_s$
choice	$_c$c	clasp	clsp
choke	$_c$k	class	cls
cholesterol	$_c$lstrl	classic	clsc
choose	$_c$os	classical	clscl
chop	$_c$p	classification	clsfc^n
chord	$_c$rd	classify	clsfy
chorus	$_c$rs	classroom	clsrm
chose	$_c$s	clay	cly / cla
Christian	$_c$rs^n	clean	cln
Christianity	$_c$rs^{nty}	cleanse	cl^c
Christmas	$_c$rsms / xmas	clear	cler
chronic	$_c$rnc / krnc	clearance	cler^c
chronicle	$_c$rncl / krncl	clearly	cler^y
chunk	$_c$nk	clerk	clrk
church	$_c$r$_c$	click	clk
cigarette	cgrt / cig	client	clnt
circle	crcl	cliff	clf
circuit	crct	climate	clmt
circulate	crclt	climb	clim
circulating	crclt^g	cling	cl^g
circulation	crcl^n	clinging	cl^{gg}
circumstance	crcmst^c	clinic	clnc / klnc
citation	cita^n	clinical	clncl
cite	ct / st	clip	clp
citizen	ctzn	clock	clk
citizenship	ctzn^p	clone	cln
city	cty	close	cls
civic	cvc	closed	clsd

closely	cls^y	coin	cn
closer	clsr	coincide	concd
closest	clst	coincidence	$concd^c$
closet	clset	cold	cld
clot	clt	collaborate	clbrt
cloth	cl_t	collaboration	$clbr^n$
clothe	clo_t	collapse	clps
clothes	$cl_t s$	collapsible	$clps^b$
clothing	cl_t^g	collar	clr
cloud	cld	collate	clt
club	clb	collated	cltd
clue	clu	colleague	cleg
cluster	clstr	collect	clct
clutch	cl_c	collectible	$clct^b$
coach	c_c	collection	clc^n
coagulate	coaglt / coag	collective	clctv
coagulation	$coagl^n/coag^n$	collector	cltr
coal	cl	college	clg / clj
coalition	$cali^n$	collision	cl^n
coast	cst	collusion	clu^n
coastal	cstl	colon	cln
coat	ct	colonial	clnl
coauthor	$cau_t r$	colony	clny
cocaine	ccan	color	clr
code	cd	colorful	clr^f
coeducation	$coedc^n$	column	clm
coeducational	$coedc^{nl}/coed$	columnist	clmst
coerce	coerc	coma	$^c a$
coerced	coercd	comatose	$^c atos$
coexist	coexst	combat	$^c bt$
coffee	cfe	combination	$^c bna^n$
cognition	cgn^n	combine	$^c bn$
cognitive	cgntv	combined	$^c bnd$
cohabit	cohbt	combustible	$^c bst^b$
coherent	cohrnt	combustion	$^c bst^n$
cohesion	coh^n	come	cm / ^{c}

comeback	cmbk / ^{c}bk
comedy	^{c}dy
comeuppance	cmup^{c} / ^{c}up^{c}
comfort	^{c}frt
comfortable	^{c}frt^{b}
comfortably	^{c}frt^{by}
comforted	^{c}frtd
comic	^{c}c
coming	cm^{g} / ^{cg}
command	^{c}nd
commanded	^{c}ndd
commander	^{c}ndr
commandment	^{c}nd^{m}
commence	cc
commencement	ccm
commencing	cg
commend	^{c}nd
commendable	^{c}nd^{b}
comment	cm
commentary	cmy
commented	cm^{d}
commenting	cmg
commerce	^{c}rs
commercial	^{c}r^{s}
commercialize	^{c}r^{s}iz
commercially	^{c}r^{sy}
commiserate	^{c}srt
commission	ç^{n}
commissioned	ç^{n}d
commissioner	ç^{n}r
commissions	ç^{n}s
commit	^{c}t
commitment	^{c}t^{m}
committee	^{c}te
commodity	^{c}odty
common	^{c}n
commonality	^{c}nlty
commonly	^{c}n^{y}
commonplace	^{c}nplc
commonsense	^{c}ns^{c}
commotion	^{c}m^{n}
communal	^{c}unl
communicable	^{c}unic^{b}
communicate	^{c}unict
communication	^{c}unic^{n}
community	^{c}unty
commute	^{c}t
compact	^{c}pct
companion	^{c}pnn
company	^{c}pny
comparability	^{c}pr^{bty}
comparable	^{c}pr^{b}
comparably	^{c}pr^{by}
compare	^{c}pr
comparison	^{c}prsn
compartment	^{c}prt^{m}
compassion	^{c}p^{n}
compel	^{c}pl
compelled	^{c}pld
compelling	^{c}pl^{g}
compensate	^{c}pnst
compensation	^{c}pns^{n}
compete	^{c}pt
competence	^{c}pt^{c}
competency	^{c}pt^{cy}
competent	^{c}ptnt
competition	^{c}pt^{n} / comp
competitive	^{c}pttv
competitor	^{c}pttr
compilation	^{c}pla^{n}
compile	^{c}pl
complain	^{c}pln

complained	^{c}plnd	computerized	^{c}ptrzd
complaint	^{c}plnt	computing	^{c}pt^g
complement	^{c}pl^m	comrade	^{c}rd
complementary	^{c}pl^{my}	comradeship	^{c}rd^p
complete	^{c}plt	concave	^{c}cv
completed	^{c}pltd	conceal	^{c}cel
completely	^{c}plt^y	concealed	^{c}celd
completion	^{c}pl^n	concede	^{c}ced
complex	^{c}plx	conceded	^{c}cedd
complexity	^{c}plxty	conceivable	^{c}cv^b
compliance	^{c}pli^c	conceivably	^{c}cv^{by}
compliant	^{c}plint	conceive	^{c}cev
complicate	^{c}plct	concentrate	^{c}cntrt
complicated	^{c}plctd	concentrated	^{c}cntrtd/concd
complication	^{c}plc^n	concentration	^{c}cntr^t / conc
complicit	^{c}plst / ^{c}plct	concept	^{c}cpt
compliment	^{c}pl^m	conception	^{c}cp^n
complimentary	^{c}pl^{my}	concepts	^{c}cpts
comply	^{c}p^y	concern	^{c}crn
component	^{c}pnt	concerned	^{c}crnd
compose	^{c}ps	concerning	^{c}crn^g
composition	^{c}ps^n	concert	^{c}crt
composure	^{c}psr	concession	^{c}s^n
compound	^{c}pnd	conciliated	^{c}cliatd
comprehend	^{c}prhnd	conciliation	^{c}clia^n
comprehension	^{c}prhn^n	conciliatory	^{c}cliat^y
comprehensive	^{c}prhnsv	concise	^{c}cs
comprise	^{c}prs	conclude	^{c}cld
comprised	^{c}prsd	concluded	^{c}cldd
compromise	^{c}prms	conclusion	^{c}cl^n
compulsion	^{c}pl^n	conclusive	^{c}clsv
compulsive	^{c}plsv	concoct	^{c}cct
compulsory	^{c}pls^y	concoction	^{c}cc^n
compunction	^{c}pnct^n	concrete	^{c}crt
computer	^{c}ptr	concur	^{c}cr
computerize	^{c}ptriz	concurred	^{c}crd

concurrence	^{c}cr^c	confidentially	^{c}fdn^{sy}
concurrent	^{c}crnt	configuration	^{c}fgr^n
concuss	^{c}cs	configure	^{c}fgr
concussion	^{c}cs^n	confine	^{c}fn
condemn	^{c}dm	confined	^{c}fnd
condemned	^{c}dmd	confinement	^{c}fn^m
condense	^{c}d^c	confirm	^{c}frm
condensed	^{c}d^{c}d	confirmation	^{c}frm^n
condescend	^{cd}nd	confirmed	^{c}frmd
condition	^{c}d^n	confiscate	^{c}fsct
conditional	^{c}d^{nl}	conflict	^{c}flct
conditionality	^{c}d^{nl}ty	conform	^{c}frm
conditioned	^{c}d^{n}d	conformed	^{c}frmd
condolence	^{c}dl^c	conforms	^{c}frms
condom	^{c}dm	confound	^{c}fnd
condone	^{c}dn	confounded	^{c}fndd
condoned	^{c}dnd	confront	^{c}frnt
conduct	^{c}dct	confrontation	^{c}frnt^n
conduit	^{c}duit	confrontational	^{c}frnt^{nl}
confection	^{c}fc^n	confuse	^{c}fs
confectionery	^{c}fc^{ny}	confusingly	^{c}fs^{gy}
confederacy	^{c}fdrcy	confusion	^{c}fs^n
confederate	^{c}fdrt	congeal	^{c}gel
confer	^{c}fr	congenial	^{c}gnial
conference	^{c}fr^c	congestion	^{c}gst^n
confess	^{c}fs	conglomerate	^{c}glmrt
confesses	^{c}fss	congratulate	^{c}grtlt
confession	^{c}f^n	congratulating	^{c}grtlt^g
confessional	^{c}fs^{nl}	congress	^{c}grs
confidant	^{c}fdnt	congressional	^{c}gr^{nl}
confide	^{c}fid	conjecture	^{c}jctur
confided	^{c}fdd	conjoined	^{c}jnd
confidence	^{c}fd^c	conjunction	^{c}jnc^n
confident	^{c}fdnt	conjure	^{c}jr
confidential	^{c}fdn^s	connect	^{c}ect
confidentiality	^{c}fdn^{s}lty	connectible	^{c}ect^b

connection	^{c}ec^n	consonant	^{c}snnt
connector	^{c}ectr	consort	^{c}srt
conqueror	^{c}qrr	consortium	^{c}srtim
conquest	^{c}qst	conspicuous	^{c}spcos
conscience	^{c}s^c	conspiracy	^{c}sprcy
conscientious	^{c}sntos	conspire	^{c}spr
conscious	^{c}sos	constable	^{c}st^b
consciously	^{c}sos^y	constabulary	^{c}stbl^y
consciousness	^{c}sosns	constant	^{c}stnt
consecutive	^{c}sctv	constantly	^{c}stnt^y
consecutively	^{c}sctv^y	constipate	^{c}stpt
consensus	^{c}snss	constituent	^{c}sttunt
consent	^{c}snt	constitute	^{c}sttut
consequence	^{c}sq^c	constitution	^{c}sttu^n
consequential	^{c}sqn^s	constitutional	^{c}sttu^{nl}
consequently	^{c}sqnt^y	constrain	^{c}strn
conservation	^{c}srv^n	constrained	^{c}strnd
conservative	^{c}srvtv	constraint	^{c}strnt
conserve	^{c}srv	constraints	^{c}strnts
consider	^{c}sdr	constrict	^{c}strct
considerable	^{c}sdr^b	construct	^{c}strct
considerably	^{c}sdr^{by}	constructed	^{c}strctd
considerate	^{c}sdrt	construction	^{c}strct^n
consideration	^{c}sdr^n	constructive	^{c}strctv
considered	^{c}sdrd	constructively	^{c}strctv^y
considers	^{c}sdrs	constructor	^{c}strctr
consignment	^{c}sn^m	construe	^{c}stru
consignments	^{c}sn^{m}s	consular	^{c}sulr
consist	^{c}st	consult	^{c}slt
consistency	^{c}st^{cy}	consultancy	^{c}slt^{cy}
consistent	^{c}stnt	consultant	^{c}sltnt
consistently	^{c}stnt^y	consultation	^{c}slt^n
consolation	^{c}sl^n	consulted	^{c}sltd
console	^{c}sl	consumable	^{c}sm^b
consolidate	^{c}sldt	consume	^{c}sm
consolidated	^{c}sldtd	consumer	^{c}smr

Word	Shorthand	Word	Shorthand
consumerism	^{c}smrsm	contributor	^{c}trbtr
consummate	^{c}smt	control	^{c}trl
consummation	^{c}sma^n	controllable	^{c}trl^b
consumption	^{c}smp^n	controls	^{c}trls
contact	^{c}tct	controversial	^{c}trv^s
contagious	^{c}tgos / ^{c}tjos	controversy	^{c}trvsy
contain	^{c}tn	conundrum	^{c}ndrm
container	^{c}tnr	conurbation	^{c}rb^n
containment	^{c}tn^m	convalesce	^{c}vls
contemplate	^{c}tmplt	convalescence	^{c}vls^c
contemporary	^{c}tmp^y	convalescent	^{c}vlsnt
contempt	^{c}tmpt	convection	^{c}vc^n
contemptible	^{c}tmpt^b	convene	^{c}vn
contend	^{c}tnd	convened	^{c}vnd
content	^{c}tnt	convenience	^{c}vni^c
contention	^{c}tn^n	convenient	^{c}vnint
contentment	^{c}tnt^m	convention	^{c}vn^n
contest	^{c}tst	conventional	^{c}vn^{nl}
contested	^{c}tstd	converged	^{c}vrgd
context	^{c}txt	convergence	^{c}vrg^c
continence	^{c}tn^c	converging	^{c}vng^g
continent	^{c}tnnt	conversant	^{c}vrsnt
contingency	^{c}tng^{cy}	conversation	^{c}vrs^n
continuation	^{c}tnu^n	converse	^{c}vrs
continue	^{c}tnu	conversely	^{c}vrs^y
continued	^{c}tnud	conversion	^{c}vr^n
continuing	^{c}tnu^g	convert	^{c}vrt
continuous	^{c}tnos	convertible	^{c}vrt^b
contract	^{c}trct	converting	^{c}vrt^g
contracted	^{c}trctd	convex	^{c}vx
contraction	^{c}trc^n	convey	^{c}vy
contractor	^{c}trctr	conveyance	^{c}vy^c
contradiction	^{c}trdc^n	convict	^{c}vct
contrast	^{c}trst	convicted	^{c}vctd
contribute	^{c}trbt	conviction	^{c}vc^n
contribution	^{c}trb^n	convince	^{c}v^c

convinced	^{c}v^{c}d	corrosion	cr^n
convincingly	^{c}vnc^{gy}	corrupt	crpt
convoluted	^{c}vltd	corruption	crp^n
convolution	^{c}vlu^n	cost	cst
convulse	^{c}vls	costed	cstd
convulsion	^{c}vl^n	costly	cst^y
cook	ck	costume	cstm
cookie	cke	cottage	ctg / ctj
cooking	ck^g	cotton	ctn
cool	cl	cough	cf
cooperate	coprt	could	cd
cooperation	copr^n	council	cncl
cooperative	coprtv / coop	counsel	cnsl
coopted	coptd	counseled	cnsld
coordinate	cordnt/coor	counseling	cnsl^g
coordinator	cordntr	counselor	cnslr
cop	cp	count	cnt
cope	cop	counter	cntr
copy	cpy	counterpart	cntrprt
copy edit	cpyedt	country	cnt^y
cord	crd	county	cnty
core	cr	coup	co
corn	crn	couple	cpl
corner	crnr	coupon	copn
coronary	crn^y	courage	crg /crj
coroner	crnr	course	crs
corporate	crprt	court	crt
corporation	crpr^n /corp	courtroom	crtrm
correct	crct	cousin	csn
correction	crc^n	covenant	cvnnt
correctly	crct^y	cover	cvr
correlate	crlt	coverage	cvrg / cvrj
correlation	crla^n	covers	cvrs
correspondence	crspnd^c	cow	cw
correspondent	crspndnt	crab	crb
corridor	crdr	crack	crk

cracked	crkd	cruel	crul
craft	crft	cruise	crs
crash	cr_s	crush	cr_s
crave	crv	crutch	cr_c
crawl	crwl	cry	c^y
crazy	crzy	crystal	crstl
cream	crem	Cuban	cbn / cu
crease	crs	cue	cu
create	crat	culminate	clmnt
creation	cra^n	culmination	$clmn^n$
creative	cratv	culpability	clp^{bty}
creativity	cratvy	culpable	clp^b
creature	crtr	cult	clt
crèche	cr_c	cultivate	cltvt
credence	crd^c	cultivation	$cltv^n$
credential	$crdn^s$	cultural	cltrl
credibility	crd^{bty}	culture	cltr
credible	crd^b	cup	cp
credit	crdt	curate	curt
creditable	$crdt^b$	curb	crb
cremation	crm^n	cure	cur
crew	crw	curiosity	crosty
crime	crm	curious	cros
criminal	crmnl	currency	cr^{cy}
crisis	crs	current	curnt
criteria	crta	currently	$crnt^y$
critic	crtc	curriculum	crclm
critical	crtcl	curtain	crtn
criticism	crtsm	curve	crv
criticize	crtcz	cushion	$c_s n$
criticized	crtczd	custody	cstdy
crocodile	crcdl / croc	custom	cstm
crop	crp	customer	cstmr
cross	crs	cut	ct
crowd	crwd	cute	cut
crowded	crwdd	cycle	ccl
crucial	cr^s		

D

dad	dd
daily	dly / d^y
dam	dm
damage	dmg / dmj
damn	dm
dance	d^c
dancer	d^{c}r
dancing	d^{cg}
danger	dngr
dangerous	dngros
dare	dr
dark	drk
darkness	drkns
dash	d$_s$
data	dta
database	dtabs
date	dt
daughter	dtr
daunt	dnt
dawn	dwn
day	dy
dead	dd
deadline	ddln
deadly	dd^y
deal	dl
dealer	dlr
dealership	dlr^p
dear	dr
death	d$_t$
debate	dbt
debated	dbtd
debrief	dbrf
debris	dbri
debt	dt
debtor	dtr
debunk	dbnk
debut	dbt
decade	dcd
decadence	dcd^c
decay	dcy
decease	dces
deceased	dcesd
deceit	dcet
deceitful	dcet^f
December	de
decent	dcnt
deception	dcp^n
decide	dcd
decided	dcdd
decimal	dcml
decision	dc^n
deck	dk
declaration	dclra^n
declare	dclr
declared	dclrd
decline	dcln
decode	dcod
decompose	dcmps
decorate	dcrt
decoration	dcr^n
decrease	dcres
dedicate	ddct
dedication	ddc^n
deduct	ddct
deductible	ddct^b
deduction	ddc^n
deem	dm
deep	dp
deepen	dpn

deeper	dpr	degradation	dgrda^n
deeply	dp^y	degrade	dgrd
deer	dr	degree	dgre
deface	dfc	dehydrate	dhydrt
defamation	dfm^n	dehydration	dhydr^n
defeat	dfet	deject	djct
defeated	dfetd	dejection	djct^n
defect	dfct	delay	dly
defective	dfctv	delayed	dlyd
defend	dfnd	delegate	dlgt
defendant	dfndnt	delegation	dlg^n
defender	dfndr	delete	dlet
defense	df^c	deletion	dl^n
defensive	df^cv	deliberate	dlbrt
defer	dfr	deliberately	dlbrt^y
deferential	dfrn^s	deliberation	dlbr^n
deferred	dfrd	delicate	dlct
defiance	dfi^c	delight	dlt
defiant	dfint	delightful	dlt^f
deficiency	dfs^{cy}	delineation	dlnea^n
deficient	dfst	deliver	dlvr
deficit	dfct	deliverable	dlvr^b
define	dfn	deliverance	dlvr^c
defined	dfnd	delivery	dlv^y
defining	dfn^g	delusion	dl^n
definite	dfnt	demand	dmnd
definitely	dfnt^y	demarcate	dmrct
definition	dfn^n	demarcation	dmrc^n
deflate	dflt	demean	dmen
deflation	dfl^n	dementia	d_ma
deforestation	dfrst^n	democracy	dmocrcy
deform	dfrm	democrat	dmocrt
deformation	dfrm^n	democratic	dmocrtc
defunct	dfnct	demographic	dmogrfc
defuse	dfus	demolish	dml_s
defy	dfy	demolition	dml^n

demonstrate	dmnstrt	deprivation	dprv^n
demonstrated	dmnstrtd	depth	dp$_t$
demonstration	dmnstr^n	deputy	dpty
demotion	dm^n	derelict	drlct
denial	dnl	dereliction	drlc^n
denigrate	dngrt	derivation	drva^n
denigration	dngr^n	derive	driv
dense	d^c	dermatology	drmt^o
density	d^{c}ty	descendant	^{d}ndnt
deny	dny	descended	^{d}ndd
depart	dprt	descends	^{d}nds
departed	dprtd	descent	^{d}nt
department	dprt^m / dpt	describable	^{d}crb^b
departmental	dprt^{ml} / dpt^{ml}	describe	^{d}crb
departure	dpftr	described	^{d}crbd
depend	dpnd / dep	description	^{d}crp^n
dependable	dpnd^b / dep^b	descriptive	^{d}crptv
dependence	dpnd^c / dep^c	desecrate	^{d}scrt
dependency	dpnd^{cy}/dep^{cy}	desecration	^{d}scr^n
dependent	dpndnt/depnt	deselect	^{d}lct
depending	dpnd^g / dep^g	deselected	^{d}lctd
depict	dpct	desert	^{d}rt
depiction	dpct^n	deserted	^{d}rtd
deplete	dplet	deserter	^{d}rtr
depletion	dpl^n	desertion	^{d}r^n
deplorable	dplr^b	deserve	^{d}rv
deplore	dplr	deserved	^{d}rvd
deploy	dply	deservedly	^{d}rvd^y
deployment	dply^m	deserves	^{d}rvs
deport	dprt	design	^{d}n
deportation	dprt^n	designate	^{d}ignt
deposit	dpst	designated	^{d}igntd
depress	dprs	designation	^{d}ign^n
depressant	dprnt	designed	^{d}ind
depressed	dprsd	designer	^{d}inr
depression	dpr^n	desirability	^{d}ir^{bty}

desirable	$^{d}ir^{b}$	destructible	$^{d}trc^{b}$
desire	^{d}ir	destruction	$^{d}trc^{n}$
desired	^{d}ird	destructive	$^{d}trctv$
desist	^{d}st	detach	dt_{c}
desisted	^{d}std	detached	$dt_{c}d$
desk	^{d}k	detachment	$dt_{c}m$
desk bound	$^{d}kbnd$	detail	dtl
desktop	^{d}ktp	detailed	$dtld$
desolate	^{d}olt	detain	dtn
desolation	$^{d}olt^{n}$	detect	$dtct$
despair	^{d}pr	detected	$dtctd$
despaired	^{d}prd	detection	dtc^{n}
despairingly	$^{d}pr^{gy}$	detective	$dtctv$
desperate	^{d}prt	detention	dtn^{n}
desperately	$^{d}prt^{y}$	deter	dtr
desperation	$^{d}pr^{n}$	determination	$dtrmn^{n}$
despicable	$^{d}pc^{b}$	determine	$dtrmn$
despicably	$^{d}pc^{by}$	determined	$dtrmnd$
despise	^{d}ps	determining	$dtrmn^{g}$
despised	^{d}psd	deterrence	dtr^{c}
despite	^{d}pt	deterring	dtr^{g}
despondency	$^{d}pnd^{cy}$	detest	$dtst$
despondent	$^{d}pndnt$	detox	dtx
dessert	^{d}rt	detoxification	$dtxfc^{n}$
destabilization	$^{d}tblz^{n}$	detract	$dtrct$
destabilize	$^{d}tblz$	detriment	dtr^{m}
destabilized	$^{d}tblzd$	detrimental	dtr^{ml}
destination	$^{d}tn^{n}$	devaluation	$dvlu^{n}$
destined	^{d}tnd	devalue	$dvlu$
destiny	^{d}tny	devastate	$dvstt$
destitute	$^{d}ttut$	devastating	$dvstt^{g}$
destitution	$^{d}ttu^{n}$	devastation	$dvst^{n}$
destroy	^{d}try	develop	dvlp/dv/dev
destroyed	$^{d}tryd$	developer	dvlpr/dvr/devr
destruct	$^{d}trct$	developing	$dvlp^{g}$/dv^{g}/dev^{g}
destructed	$^{d}trctd$		

development	dvlp^m /dv^m / dev^m	differently	dfrnt^y
		difficult	dfclt / dif
developmental	dvlp^{ml} /dv^{ml} / dev^{ml}	difficulty	dfclty
		diffidence	dfd^c
deviate	dvit	diffident	dfdnt
deviation	dvi^n	diffuse	dfus
device	dvc	dig	dg
devil	dvl	digest	dgst
devolution	dvlu^n	digestion	dgst^n
devolve	dvlv	digital	dgtl
devote	dvt	dignity	dgnty
devotion	dv^n	dilate	dlat
diabetes	dibts	dilation	dla^n
diagnose	diagns	dilemma	dlma
diagnosis	diagnss	diligence	dlg^c
diagram	diagrm / dia	dimension	dmn^n
dial	dil	diminish	dmn$_s$
dialect	dialct	dining	dn^g
dialogue	dialg	dinner	dnr
dialysis	dialss	dinosaur	dnosr / dino
dialyzing	dialz^g	diplomat	dplomt
diamond	dimnd	diplomatic	dplomtc
diaphragm	diphm/diafrm	direct	drct
diarrhea	diarea	direction	drc^n
diary	di^y	directly	drct^y
dictate	dctt	director	drctr / dir
dictation	dct^n	directory	drct^y
diction	dc^n	dirt	drt
dictionary	dc^{ny}	dirty	drty
did	dd	disabilities	^{db}ts
die	di	disability	^{db}ty
diet	diet	disable	^{db}
dietitian	diet^n	disabled	^{db}d
differ	dfr	disablement	^{db}m
difference	dfr^c	disables	^{db}s
different	dfrnt		

disadvantage	^{d}advntg / ^{d}advntj	disciplinary	^{d}pln^y
		discipline	^{d}pln
disadvantaged	^{d}advntgd	disciplined	^{d}plnd
disadvantages	^{d}advntgs	disclose	^{d}cls
disaffect	^{d}afct	disclosed	^{d}clsd
disaffected	^{d}afctd	disclosure	^{d}clsr
disaffection	^{d}afc^n	discolor	^{d}clr
disagree	^{d}agre	discolored	^{d}clrd
disagreeable	^{d}agr^b	discomfort	^{dc}frt
disagreeably	^{d}agr^{by}	disconcerting	^{dc}crt^g
disagreed	^{d}agrd	disconcertingly	^{dc}crt^{gy}
disagreement	^{d}agr^m	disconnect	^{dc}ct
disallow	^{d}alw	disconnected	^{dc}ctd
disappear	^{d}apr	discontent	^{dc}tnt
disappearance	^{d}apr^c	discontented	^{dc}tntd
disappeared	^{d}aprd	discontinue	^{dc}tnu
disappoint	^{d}apnt	discontinued	^{dc}tnud
disappointed	^{d}apntd	discount	^{d}cnt
disappointment	^{d}apnt^m	discountable	^{d}cnt^b
disapproval	^{d}aprvl	discounted	^{d}cntd
disapprove	^{d}aprv	discourage	^{d}crg / ^{d}crj
disapproved	^{d}aprvd	discouragement	^{d}crg^m
disapprovingly	^{d}aprv^{gy}	discourse	^{d}crs
disarray	^{d}ary	discourtesy	^{d}crtsy
disassociate	^{d}ascit	discover	^{d}cvr
disaster	^{d}astr	discoverable	^{d}cvr^b
disband	^{d}bnd	discovered	^{d}cvrd
disbanded	^{d}bndd	discovery	^{d}cv^y
disbelief	^{d}blf	discredit	^{d}crdt
disc	^{d}c / dsc	discredited	^{d}crdtd
discard	^{d}crd	discrepancy	^{d}crp^{cy}
discarded	^{d}crdd	discretion	^{d}cr^n
discern	^{d}rn	discretionary	^{d}cr^{ny}
discernible	^{d}rn^b	discrimination	^{d}crmn^n
discharge	^{d}crg	discuss	^{d}cs
discharged	^{d}crgd	discussed	^{d}csd

discussion	^{d}c^n	disk	^{d}k
disdain	^{d}sdn	dislike	^{d}lk
disease	^{d}es	dislikeable	^{d}lk^b
diseased	^{d}esd	disliked	^{d}lkd
disengage	^{d}engg/^{d}engj	dislikes	^{d}lks
disengaged	^{d}enggd	dislocate	^{d}lct
disengagement	^{d}engg^m	dislocated	^{d}lctd
disentangle	^{d}entngl	dislodge	^{d}lg / ^{d}lj
disfigure	^{d}fgr	dislodged	^{d}lgd
disfigured	^{d}fgrd	disloyal	^{d}lyl
disfigurement	^{d}fgr^m	disloyalty	^{d}lylty
disgrace	^{d}grc	dismiss	^{d}ms
disgraced	^{d}grcd	disorder	^{d}ordr
disgraceful	^{d}grc^f	disparage	^{d}prg / ^{d}prj
disgracefully	^{d}grc^{fy}	disparity	^{d}prty
disguise	^{d}gis	dispatch	^{d}p$_c$
disguised	^{d}gsd	dispatched	^{d}p$_c$d
disguises	^{d}gss	dispatches	^{d}p$_c$s
disgust	^{d}gst	dispel	^{d}pl
disgusted	^{d}gstd	dispelled	^{d}pld
dish	d$_s$	dispensary	^{d}pns^y
disheveled	^d_svld	dispensation	^{d}pns^n
dishonest	^{d}hnst	dispense	^{d}p^c
dishonestly	^{d}hnst^y	dispersal	^{d}prsl
disillusion	d$_i$l^n	disperse	^{d}prs
disillusioned	d$_i$l^{n}d	displace	^{d}plc
disillusionment	d$_i$l^{nm}	displaced	^{d}plcd
disinfect	^{d}infct	display	^{d}ply / ^{d}pla
disinfectant	^{d}infctnt	displayed	^{d}plyd
disinfected	^{d}infctd	displease	^{d}pls
disintegrate	^{d}ingrt	disposable	^{d}ps^b
disintegrated	^{d}ingrtd	disposal	^{d}psl
disintegration	^{d}ingr^n	dispose	^{d}ps
disinterest	^{d}intrst	disposition	^{d}ps^n
disjointed	^{d}jntd	dispossess	^{d}pss
		dispossessed	^{d}pssd

disproportion	$^{d}ppr^{n}$	dissolve	^{d}lv
disproportional	$^{d}ppr^{nl}$	dissolved	^{d}lvd
disproportionate	$^{d}ppr^{n}t$	dissuade	^{d}uad
disproportionately	$^{d}ppr^{nty}$	dissuaded	$^{d}uadd$
disprove	^{d}prv	distance	$^{d}t^{c}$
disputable	$^{d}pt^{b}$	distanced	$^{d}t^{c}d$
disputably	$^{d}pt^{by}$	distances	$^{d}t^{c}s$
dispute	^{d}pt	distant	^{d}nt
disputed	^{d}ptd	distantly	$^{d}nt^{y}$
disqualification	$^{d}qlfc^{n}$	distaste	^{d}tst
disqualified	$^{d}qlfd$	distasteful	$^{d}tst^{f}$
disqualify	$^{d}qlfy$	distinct	$^{d}tnct$
disregard	$^{d}rgrd$	distinction	$^{d}tnc^{n}$
disregarded	$^{d}rgrdd$	distinctive	$^{d}tnctv$
disrepair	^{d}rpr	distinctiveness	$^{d}tnctvns$
disreputable	$^{d}rpt^{b}$	distinctly	$^{d}tnct^{y}$
disrepute	$^{d}rput$	distinctness	$^{d}tnctns$
disrespect	$^{d}rspct$	distinguish	$^{d}tngi_{s}$
disrespectful	$^{d}rspct^{f}$	distinguishable	$^{d}tng_{s}^{b}$
disrupt	^{d}rpt	distinguished	$^{d}tng_{s}d$
disrupted	$^{d}rptd$	distort	^{d}trt
disruption	$^{d}rp^{n}$	distortion	$^{d}tr^{n}$
disruptive	$^{d}rptv$	distract	$^{d}trct$
dissatisfaction	$^{d}stsfc^{n}$	distracted	$^{d}trctd$
dissatisfactory	$^{d}stsfct^{y}$	distractedly	$^{d}trctd^{y}$
dissatisfied	$^{d}stsfd$	distraction	$^{d}trc^{n}$
dissatisfy	$^{d}stsfy$	distracts	$^{d}trcts$
disseminate	$^{d}smnat$	distraught	^{d}trt
disseminated	$^{d}smntd$	distress	^{d}trs
dissension	$^{d}n^{n}$	distressed	$^{d}trsd$
dissent	^{d}nt	distressful	$^{d}trs^{f}$
dissented	^{d}ntd	distribute	$^{d}trbt$
dissertation	$^{d}rt^{n}$	distributed	$^{d}trbtd$
disservice	^{d}rvc	distributes	$^{d}trbts$
dissimilar	^{d}mlr	distribution	$^{d}trb^{n}$
dissolution	$^{d}lu^{n}$		

district	^{d}trct	documentary	dc^{my}
distrust	^{d}trst	dodge	dj
distrusted	^{d}trstd	does	ds
distrustful	^{d}trst^f	doesn't	dsnt
disturb	^{d}trb	dog	dg
disturbance	^{d}trb^c	doing	d^g
disturbances	^{d}trb^{c}s	doll	dl
disturbed	^{d}trbd	dollar	dlr
disturbing	^{d}trb^g	dolphin	dlfn
disturbingly	^{d}trb^{gy}	domain	dmn
disturbs	^{d}trbs	domestic	dmstc
disused	^{d}usd	dominant	dmnnt
dither	d$_t$r	dominate	dmnt
diverge	dvrg	dominating	dmnt^g
divergence	dvrg^c	domination	dmn^n
divergent	dvrgnt	domineer	dmner
diverse	dvrs	don't	dnt
diversify	dvrsfy	donate	dnat
diversion	dvr^n	donation	dn^n
diversity	dvrsty	done	dn
divide	÷ / dvd	donor	dnr
divided	÷d / dvdd	door	dr
dividing	÷^{g} / dvd^g	doorway	drwy
divine	dvn	dose	ds / dos
divisible	÷^{b} / dvs^b	dot	dt / .
division	÷n / dv^n	double	dbl / x2
divorce	dvrc	doubt	dbt
divorced	dvrcd	doubtful	dt^f
divulge	dvlg	dough	doh
DNA	dna	down	dn
do	do / d	downgrade	dngrd
doable	d^b	downgraded	dngrdd
dock	dk	download	dnld
doctor	dctr / dr	downloaded	dnldd
doctrine	dctrn	downplay	dnply
document	dc^m / doc	downsize	dnsz

downtown	dntn	duck	dk
dozen	dzn	due	du
draft	drft	dumb	dmb
drag	drg	dump	dmp
dragon	drgn	duplicate	dplct
drain	drn	duplication	dplc^n
drama	drma	durable	dr^b
dramatic	drmtc	duration	dra^n
dramatically	drmtc^y	duress	drs
draw	drw	during	dr^g
drawback	drwbck	dust	dst
drawer	drwr	Dutch	d$_c$
drawing	drw^g	dutiful	dti^f
drawn	drwn	duty	dty
dreadful	drd^f	dwelling	dwl^g
dream	drm	dye	dy / di
drench	drn$_c$	dying	dy^g
dress	drs	dynamic	dnmc
dried	drd	dynamics	dnmcs
drift	drft	dyscalculia	^{d}clcla
drill	drl	dysfunction	^{d}fnc^n
drink	drnk	dysfunctional	^{d}fnc^{nl}
drinkable	drnk^b	dyslexia	^{d}lxa
drinking	drnk^g	dyspraxia	^{d}prxa
drive	drv		
driven	drvn		
driver	drvr		
driveway	drvwy		
driving	drv^g		
drop	drp		
drown	drwn		
drug	drg		
drum	drm		
drummer	drmr		
drunk	drnk		
dry	d^y		

E

each	e_c
eager	egr
eagle	egl
ear	er
early	er^y
earmark	ermrk
earn	ern / urn
earning	ern^g
earnings	ern^{g}s
earshot	er$_s$t
earth	er$_t$
earthquake	er$_t$qk
ease	es
easement	es^m
easily	es^y
east	est
Easter	estr
eastern	estrn
easy	esy / ec
eat	et
eating	et^g
echo	e_co
ecological	e^o_ccl
ecology	ec^o
economic	ecnmc
economically	ecnmc^y
economics	ecnmcs
economist	ecnmst
economize	ecnmz
economy	ecnmy /econ
ecosystem	ecsstm
eczema	exma
edge	ej
edible	ed^b
edit	edt
edition	ed^n
editor	edtr
educate	edct
education	edc^n / edu
educational	edc^{nl}
educator	edctr
effect	efct
effective	efctv
effectively	efctv^y
effectiveness	efctvns
efficiency	ef^{cy}
efficient	efcnt
effluence	eflu^c
effort	efrt
egg	eg
ego	ego
eight	8
eighteen	18
eighth	8th / 8$_t$
eighty	80
either	e_tr
eject	ejct
elaborate	elbrt
elapse	elaps
elapsed	elapsd
elation	ela^n
elbow	elbo
elder	eldr
elderly	eldr^y
elect	elct
elected	elctd
election	elc^n

electric	elctrc	embrace	embrc
electrical	elctrcl / elec	emerge	emrg
electrician	$eltr^n$ / $elec^n$	emergence	$emrg^c$
electricity	elctrcty	emergency	$emrg^{cy}$
electronic	elctrnc	emerging	$emrg^g$
electronics	elctrncs	emigration	$emgra^n$
elegance	elg^c	eminence	emn^c
elegant	elgnt	eminent	emnnt
element	el^m	emission	em^n
elemental	el^{ml}	emotion	emo^n
elementary	el^{my}	emotional	emo^{nl}
elephant	elfnt	emotionally	emo^{ny}
elevate	elvt	empathize	$emp_t z$
elevation	elv^n	empathy	$emp_t y$
elevator	elvtr	emperor	empr
eleven	11	emphasis	emphss/emfss
eleventh	11th / 11_t	emphasize	emphsiz
eligible	elg^b	empire	empr
eliminate	elmnat	employ	emply
elimination	$elmn^n$	employable	$emply^b$
elite	elt	employee	emplye
elongate	elngt	employment	$emply^m$
elongation	$elnga^n$	empower	empwr
eloquence	elq^c	empty	empt / mpt
eloquent	elqnt	emulate	emult
else	els	enable	en^b
elsewhere	$els_w r$	enact	enct
email	eml	enactment	$enct^m$
embankment	$embnk^m$	encampment	$encmp^m$
embargo	embrgo	enclose	encls / enc
embarrass	embrs	enclosed	enclsd / encd
embarrassed	embrsd	enclosure	enclsr
embassy	embsy/embsc	encounter	encntr
embezzle	embzl	encourage	encrg / encrj
embodiment	$embdi^m$	encouraging	$encrg^g$
embody	embdy	encroach	$encr_c$

encrypt	encrpt	enter	e
encrypted	encrptd	entered	^{e}d
encryption	encrp^n	enterprise	^{e}prs
end	nd	entertain	^{e}tn
endeavor	endvr	entertainment	^{e}tn^m
endless	endls	enthusiasm	en$_t$sism
endorse	endrs	enthusiastic	en$_t$sitc
endorsed	endrsd	entire	entr
endorsement	endrs^m	entirely	entr^y
endoscopy	enscpy	entitle	enttl
endow	endw	entitlement	enttl^m
endowment	endw^m	entity	enty
endurance	endr^c	entrance	entr^c
endure	endr	entrap	entrp
enemy	enmy	entrepreneur	entrprnr
energy	enrgy	entry	ent^y
enforce	enfrc	envelope	envlp
enforcement	enfrc^m	environment	envrn^m
engage	engg / engj	environmental	envrn^{ml}
engagement	engg^m	envision	env^n
engine	engn	epidemic	epdmc
engineer	engnr	epidermis	epdrms
engineering	engnr^g	epidural	epdrl
English	engl$_s$ / eng	episode	epsd
engulf	englf	equal / s	=
enhance	enh^c	equality	eqlty
enjoy	enjy	equally	eq^y
enjoyable	enjy^b	equate	eqt
enjoyment	enjy^m	equation	eq^n
enlarge	enlrg	equip	eqp
enlargement	enlrg^m	equipment	eqp^m
enormous	enrmos	equity	eqty
enough	enf	equivalent	eqvlnt
enroll	enrl	era	era
enrollment	enrl^m	eradicate	erdct
ensure	en$_s$r	eradication	erdc^n

erase	eras	evaluate	evlut
erect	erct	evaluation	evlu^n
erection	erc^n	evaporate	evprt
erode	erod	evaporation	evpor^n
erosion	er^n	even	evn
error	err	evening	evn^g
escalate	esclt	event	evnt
escalating	esclt^g	eventful	evnt^f
escape	escp	eventually	evnt^y
Eskimo	eskmo	ever	evr
especially	esp^{sy}	evergreen	evgrn
essay	esy	everlasting	evrlst^g
essence	es^c	every	ev^y
essential	esn^s	everybody	ev^{y}bdy
essentially	esn^{sy}	everyday	ev^{y}dy
establish	estbl$_s$	everyone	ev^{y}on / ev^{y}1
established	estbl$_s$d	everything	ev^y_tg
establishment	estbl$_s^m$	everywhere	ev^y_wr
estate	estt	evict	evct
estimate	estmt / est	evicted	evctd
estimated	estmtd / estd	eviction	evc^n
estimation	estm^n	evidence	evd^c
etc	etc	evident	evdnt
etch	e$_c$	evidential	evdn^s
ethic	e$_t$c	evil	evl
ethical	e$_t$cl	evolution	evl^n
ethics	e$_t$cs	evolve	evlv
ethnic	e$_t$nc	exact	xct
ethnicity	e$_t$ncty	exactly	xct^y
ethos	e$_t$s	exam	xm
etiquette	etqt	examination	xmn^n
Europe	erop	examine	xmn
European	eropn	examined	xmnd
evacuate	evcut	examiner	xmnr
evacuation	evcu^n	example	xmpl / ex
evade	evd		

excavate	xcvt	exert	xrt
excavation	xcv^n	exerting	xrt^g
exceed	xcd	exertion	xr^n
excel	xl	exhale	xhl
excellence	xl^c	exhaust	xhst
excellent	xlnt	exhaustion	xhst^n
except	xcpt	exhibit	xhbt
exception	xcp^n	exhibition	xhb^n
exceptional	xcp^{nl}	exist	xst
excess	xcs	existence	xst^c
excessive	xsv	existing	xst^g
exchange	x$_c$ng	exit	xt
exchanged	x$_c$ngd	ex-officio	x-ofco
excitable	xcit^b	exonerate	xonr
excite	xcit	exonerated	xonrtd
excited	xcitd	exorbitant	xrbtnt
excitement	xcit^m	exotic	xotc
exciting	xcit^g	expand	xpnd
exclaimed	xclmd	expandable	xpnd^b
exclamation	xclm^n / !	expansion	xpn^n
exclude	xcld	expect	xpct
exclusion	xcl^n	expectation	xpct^n
exclusive	xclsv	expected	xpctd
exclusively	xclsv^y	expedient	xpdint
excrement	xcr^m	expedition	xpd^n
excursion	xcr^n	expendable	xpnd^b
excusable	xcs^b	expense	xp^c
excuse	xcs / xcus	expenses	xp^{c}s
excused	xcsd	expensive	xpnsv
execute	xct	experience	xpr^c
execution	xc^n	experienced	xpr^{c}d
executive	xctv / exec	experiment	xpri^m
exempt	xmpt	experimental	xpri^{ml}
exercise	xrcis / exer	expert	xprt
exercised	xrcisd	expertise	xprtis
exercising	xrcis^g	expiration	xpr^n

expire	xpr
explain	xpln
explained	xplnd
explanation	xpln^n
explicable	xplc^b
explicit	xplct
exploit	xplot
exploration	xplr^n
explore	xplr
explosion	xpl^n
export	xprt
expose	xps
exposure	xpsr
express	xprs
expression	xpr^n
expulsion	xpl^n
extend	xtnd
extended	xtndd
extension	xtn^n
extensive	xtnsv
extent	xtnt
extenuating	xtnut^g
external	xtrnl
extortionate	xtr^nt
extra	xtra
extract	xtrct
extraction	xtrc^n
extradite	xtrdit
extradition	xtrd^n
extraordinary	xtrordn^y
extreme	xtrm
extremely	xtrm^y
exuberance	xubr^c
eye	i
eyebrow	ibrw

F

fable	f^b
fabric	fbrc
fabrication	fbrc^n
face	fc / fs
facelift	fclft
facial	f^s
facilitate	fcltt
facilities	fclts
facility	fclty
fact	fct
factor	fctr
factory	fct^y
faculty	fclty
fade	fd
fail	fl / fal
failure	flr
faint	fnt
fair	fr
fairly	fr^y
faith	f_t
faithful	$\text{f}_t^{\ f}$
fall	fl
fallible	fl^b
false	fls
falsify	flsfy
fame	fm
familial	fmlil
familiar	fmlir
family	fm^y / fam
famous	fmos
fan	fn

Word	Shorthand	Word	Shorthand
fantastic	fntstc	feedback	fdbk
fantasy	fntsy	feel	fl / fel
far	fr	feeling	fl^g
fare	fr / far	fees	fs
farm	frm	feet	ft / fet
farmer	frmr	fell	fl
fascinate	fsnt	fellow	flw /flo
fascinating	fsnt^g	fellowship	flw^p
fascination	fsa^n	felt	flt
fashion	f$_s$n	female	fml / F / ♀
fashionable	f$_s$n^b	feminist	fmnst
fast	fst	fence	f^c
faster	fstr	fencing	f^{cg}
fat	ft	ferment	fr^m
fatal	ftl	festival	fstvl
fate	ft / fat	fetch	f$_c$
fateful	ft^f	fever	fvr
father	f$_t$r	few	fw
fatigue	ftig	fewer	fwr
fattening	ftn^g	fiber	fbr
fault	flt	fickle	fkl
faulty	flty	fiction	fc^n
favor	fvr	field	fld
favorable	fvr^b	fierce	frc
favorite	fvrt	fifteen	15
fax	fx	fifth	5th / 5$_t$
fear	fr	fifty	50
feasible	fs^b	fight	ft
feather	f$_t$r	fighter	ftr
feature	ftr	fighting	ft^g
February	fe	figure	fgr
federal	fdrl	figures	fgrs
federate	fdrt	file	fil
federation	fdr^n	fill	fl
fee	fe	film	flm
feed	fd		

filter	fltr	flatlining	fltln^g
fin	fn	flatten	fltn
final	fnl	flatter	fltr
finalize	fnliz	flatulence	fltul^c
finally	fn^y	flavor	flvr
finance	fn^c	flee	fle
financial	fnn^s	fleet	flt
find	fnd	flesh	fl$_s$
finding	fnd^g	flex	flx
fine	fn / fin	flexibility	flx^{bty}
finger	fngr	flexible	flx^b
finish	fn$_s$	flight	flt
fire	fr	flinch	fln$_c$
firm	frm	fling	fl^g
firmly	frm^y	flip	flp
first	frst / 1st	float	flt /flot
fiscal	fscl	flood	fld
fish	f$_s$	floor	flr
fisherman	f$_s$rmn	flotation	flot^n
fishing	f$_s$^{g}	flour	flr
fist	fst	flourish	flr$_s$
fistful	fst^f	flouting	flot^g
fit	ft	flow	flo
fitful	ft^f	flower	flwr
fitness	ftns	fluctuate	flctut
five	5	fluctuation	flctu^n
fix	fx	fluid	flid
fixation	fxa^n	fly	f^y
fixed	fxd	flying	f^{yg}
flag	flg	focus	fcs
flagship	flg^p	fog	fg
flamboyant	flmbynt	fold	fld
flame	flm	folk	flk
flamingo	flmngo	follow	flw / flo
flash	fl$_s$	following	flw^g
flat	flt	font	fnt

food	fod / fd	foretell	^{f}tl / 4tl
fool	fol / fl	foretold	^{f}tld / 4tld
foot	fot / ft	forever	^{f}evr / 4evr
football	ftbl	forewarn	^{f}wrn / 4wrn
for	^{f} / 4	forfeit	^{f}ft / 4ft
for example	eg	forfeited	^{f}ftd / 4ftd
for information	4 info / ^{f}infrm^n / ^{f}info	forfeiture	^{f}ftr / 4ftr
forbid	^{f}bd / 4bd	forge	^{f}g / 4g
forbidden	^{f}bdn / 4dbn	forged	^{f}gd / 4gd
force	^{f}c / 4c	forget	^{f}gt / 4gt
forced	^{f}cd / 4cd	forgetful	^{f}gt^f / 4gt^f
forceful	^{f}c^f / 4c^f	forgettable	^{f}gt^b / 4gt^b
forcefully	^{f}c^{fy} / 4c^{fy}	forgivable	^{f}gv^b / 4gv^b
forcible	^{f}c^b / 4c^b	forgive	^{f}gv / 4gv
forcibly	^{f}c^{by} / 4c^{by}	forgiveness	^{f}gvns / 4gvns
foreboding	^{f}bd^g / 4bd^g	forgo	^{f}go / 4go
forecast	^{f}cst / 4cst	forgot	^{f}gt / 4gt
forecaster	^{f}cstr / 4cstr	forgotten	^{f}gtn / 4gtn
foreclose	^{f}cls / 4cls	fork	^{f}k / 4k
foreclosure	^{f}clsr / 4clsr	form	^{f}m / 4m
forefront	^{f}frnt / 4frnt	formal	^{f}ml / 4ml
forehead	^{f}fhd / 4hd	formalize	^{f}mlz / 4mlz
foreign	^{f}n / 4n	formally	^{f}m^y / 4m^y
foreigner	^{f}nr / 4nr	format	^{f}mt / 4mt
foreigners	^{f}nrs / 4nrs	formation	^{f}m^n / 4m^n
foreman	^{f}mn / 4mn	formed	^{f}md / 4md
forename	^{f}nm / 4nm	former	^{f}mr / 4mr
forensic	^{f}nsc / 4nsc	formerly	^{f}mr^y / 4mr^y
forerunner	^{f}rnr / 4rnr	formula	^{f}mla / 4mla
foresaw	^{f}sw / 4sw	formulate	^{f}mlt / 4mlt
foresee	^{f}se / 4nrse	formulation	^{f}mul^n / 4mul^n
foreseeable	^{f}se^b / 4se^b	fort	^{f}t / 4t
foresight	^{f}st / 4st	forth	^f_t / 4_t
forest	^{f}est / 4est	forthcoming	^f_tcm^g / 4_tcm^g
foretaste	^{f}tst / 4tst	fortify	^{f}tfy / 4tfy

fortnight	^{f}tnt / 4tnt	freeze	frz
fortunate	^{f}tunt / 4tunt	French	frn$_c$ / fr
fortunately	^{f}tunt^y / 4tunt^y	frequency	frq^{cy}
fortune	^{f}tun / 4tun	frequent	frqnt
forty	40	frequently	frqnt^y
forum	^{f}um / 4um	fresh	fr$_s$
forward	^{f}wd / 4wd	freshman	fr$_s$mn
forwarded	^{f}wdd / 4wdd	friction	frc^n
foster	fstr	Friday	fr
found	fnd	friend	frnd
foundation	fnd^n	friendly	frnd^y
founder	fndr	friendship	frnd^p
four	4	fright	frt
fourteen	14	frightening	frtn^g
fourth	fr$_t$ / 4th / 4$_t$	frightful	frt^f
fox	fx	frog	frg
fraction	frc^n	from	frm
fractional	frc^{nl}	front	frnt
fracture	frctr	frontier	frntr
fragile	frgl	froth	fr$_t$
fragment	frg^m	frown	frwn
fragmented	frg^{m}d	frozen	frzn
fragrance	frgr^c	fruit	frt
fragrant	frgrt	fruitful	frt^f
frame	frm / fram	fruition	frui^n
framework	frmwrk	frustrate	frstrt
franchise	frn$_c$s	frustration	frstr^n
frankly	frnk^y	fucking	fk^g
fraud	frd	fuel	ful
fraudulent	frdlnt	fulfill	flfl
fraught	fraut	fulfillment	flfl^m
free	fre	full	fl
freedom	frdm	full-time	fltm
freelance	frl^c	fully	f^y
freely	fre^y	fun	fn
freeway	frewy	function	fnc^n

functional	fnc^{nl}		
fund	fnd		
fundamental	fnd^{ml}		
fundamentally	fnd^{my}		
funding	fnd^{g}		
fundraising	fndrs^{g}		
funds	fnds		
funeral	fnrl		
fur	fr		
furnish	frn$_{s}$		
furniture	frntr		
further	fr$_{t}$r		
furthermore	fr$_{t}$rmr		
fusion	f^{n}		
futile	ftl		
future	ftr / ftur		

G

gain	gn		
galaxy	glxy		
gallery	gl^{y}		
gamble	gmbl		
game	gm		
gang	gng		
gap	gp		
garage	grg / grj		
garbage	grbg / grbj		
garden	grdn		
garlic	grlc		
garment	gr^{m}		
gas	gs		
gasoline	gsln		
gastric	gstrc		
gate	gt		
gather	g$_{t}$r		
gathering	g$_{t}$r^{g}		
gave	gv		
gay	gy / ga		
gaze	gz		
gear	gr		
gender	gndr		
gene	gn		
general	gnrl		
generally	gnr^{y}		
generate	gnrt		
generation	gnr^{n}		
generic	gnrc		
generous	gnros		
genetic	gntc		
genius	gnus		

genre	gnr	goat	got /gt
gentle	gntl	God	gd
gentleman	gntlmn	going	g^g
gently	gnt^y	gold	gld
genuine	gnin	golden	gldn
gerbil	grbl	golf	glf
German	grmn / gr	gone	gn
gesture	gstr	good	gd
get	gt	gorilla	grla
ghost	gst	got	gt
giant	gnt /gint	govern	gvrn
gibbon	gbn	governance	gvrn^c
gift	gft	government	gvrn^m / gov
gifted	gftd	governor	gvrnr
gimmick	gmk	grab	grb
giraffe	grf	grace	grc
girl	grl	graceful	grc^f
girlfriend	grlfrnd	grade	grd
girth	gr$_t$	gradual	grdul
give	gv	gradually	grdu^y
given	gvn	graduate	grdut / grad
glad	gld	graduation	grdu^n
glamour	glmr	graft	grft
glance	gl^c	grain	grn
glare	glr	grand	grnd
glass	gls	grandchild	grnd$_c$ld
glimpse	glmps	grandfather	grndf$_t$r
glint	glnt	grandmother	grndm$_t$r
glitch	gl$_c$	grandparent	grndprnt
global	glbl	grant	grnt
globe	glb	grape	grp
glory	gl^y	graph	grf
glove	glv	graphical	grfcl
glucose	glcs	grasp	grsp
go	go / g	grass	grs
goal	gol / gl	grateful	grt^f

gratis	grts	guide	gd
grave	grv	guideline	gdln
gravel	grvl	guilt	glt
gravitate	grvtt	guilty	glty
gravitation	grvt^n	guitar	gtr /gitr
gravity	grvty	gullible	gl^b
gravy	grvy	gun	gn
gray	gry	gut	gt
great	grt	guy	gy
greater than	>	gym	gm
greatest	grtst / >	gynecology	gnc^o / gyn
greatly	grt^y		
Greek	grk / gr		
green	grn		
greet	gret		
grew	grw		
grief	grf		
grievance	grv^c		
grieve	grv		
grin	grn		
grip	grp		
grocery	grc^y		
groom	grm		
gross	grs		
ground	grnd		
group	grp		
grow	grw / gro		
growing	grw^g / gro^g		
growth	grw$_t$		
grueling	gruel^g		
guarantee	grnte		
guard	grd		
guardian	grdian		
guess	gs		
guest	gst		
guidance	gd^c		

H

ha	ha
habit	hbt
habitable	hbt^b
habitat	hbtt
habitation	hbt^n
had	hd
hair	hr
hairdresser	hrdrsr
half	hlf / 1/2 / .5
halfway	hlfwy /1/2wy
hall	hl
hallmark	hlmrk
hallway	hlwy
hammer	hmr
hamster	hmstr
hand	hnd
handful	hnd^f
handle	hndl
handover	hndovr/hnd^o
handsome	hndsm
handwriting	hndrt^g
hang	hng
happen	hpn
happened	hpnd
happily	hp^y
happiness	hpns / hpins
happy	hpy
harass	hras
harassment	hras^m
harbor	hrbr
hard	hrd

harden	hrdn
hardly	hrd^y
hardship	hrd^p
hardware	hrdwr
hardy	hrdy
harm	hrm
harmful	hrm^f
harmony	hrmny
harsh	hr$_s$
harvest	hrvst
has	hs
hat	ht
hatch	h$_c$
hate	ht / hat
hateful	ht^f
haul	hl /hal
hauler	hlr
have	hv
hay	hy /ha
hazard	hzrd
hazardous	hzrds/hzrdos
hazel	hzl
he	h
head	hd
headache	hda$_c$
headhunted	hdhntd
headhunter	hdhntr
headhunting	hdhnt^g
headline	hdln
headquarters	hdqtrs
headship	hd^p
heal	hl
health	hl$_t$
health-care	hl$_t$cr
healthy	hl$_t$y
hear	hr

heard	hrd	hide	hid
hearing	hr^g	hierarchy	hirr$_c$y / hirrky
heart	hrt	high	hi
heat	ht	highlight	hilt
heaven	hvn	highly	hi^y
heavily	hv^y	high-tech	hi-t$_c$ / hi-tk
heavy	hvy	highway	hiwy
hedge	hj / hg	hike	hk
heel	hl /hel	hill	hl
height	ht	him	hm
held	hld	himself	hmslf
helicopter	hlcptr /heli	hinder	hndr
hell	hl	hindrance	hndr^c
hello	hlo / hi	Hindu	hndu
helmet	hlmt	hint	hnt
help	hlp	hip	hp
helpdesk	hlpdsk	hire	hir
helpful	hlp^f	his	hs
hence	h^c	Hispanic	hspnc / hisp
her	hr	historian	hstrn
herb	hrb	historic	hstrc
here	hr / her	historical	hstrcl
heredity	hrdty	historically	hstrc^y
heritage	hrtg / hrtj	history	hst^y
hero	hro	hit	ht
heroine	hron	hitch	h$_c$
hers	hrs	hoard	hord
herself	hrslf	hockey	hky
hesitance	hst^c	hold	hld
hesitancy	hst^{cy}	hole	hl / hol
hesitant	hstnt	holiday	hldy
hesitate	hstt	hollow	hlo
hesitation	hst^n	holly	h^y / ho^y
hey	hy	holy	h^y
hi	hi	home	hm
hidden	hdn	homecoming	hmcm^g

homeland	hmlnd	hug	hg
homeless	hmls	huge	hj / hg
homework	hmwrk	huh	h
honest	hnst	human	hmn
honestly	hnst^y	human resources	hr / HR
honey	hny	humanity	hmnty
honor	hnr	humble	hm^b
honorable	hnr^b	humiliate	hmlit
hook	hk	humiliation	hmli^n
hope	hp	humor	hmr
hoped	hpd	hundred	100
hopeful	hp^f	hunger	hngr
hopefully	hp^{fy}	hungry	hng^y
horizon	hrzn	hunt	hnt
hormone	hrmn	hunter	hntr
horn	hrn	hunting	hnt^g
horrible	hr^b	hurricane	hrcn
horribly	hr^{by}	hurry	h^y
horrify	hrfy	hurt	hrt
horror	hrr	hurtful	hrt^f
horse	hrs	husband	hsbnd /hubi
hospitable	hspt^b	hydration	hdr^n
hospital	hsptl / hsp	hyperactive	hpractv/^{h}actv
host	hst	hypersensitive	hprsnstv / ^{h}snstv
hostage	hstg /hstj		
hostel	hstl	hypertension	hprtn^n / ^{h}tn^n
hostile	hostl	hyposensitive	hposnstv / $_h$snstv
hot	ht		
hotel	htl	hypotension	hpotn^n/$_h$tn^n
hour	hr	hypothesis	hpo$_t$s / $_{ht}$s
hours	hrs	hypothetical	hpo$_t$tcl / $_{ht}$tcl
house	hs		
household	hshld		
housing	hs^g		
how	hw		
however	hwevr		

I

I	i
ice	ic
ice cream	ic crm
icon	icn
idea	ida
ideal	idel
idealize	idelz
identical	idntcl
identification	idntfc^n / id
identified	idntfd
identifies	idntfs
identify	idntfy
identity	idntty
ideological	id^{o}cl
ideology	id^o
ie	ie
if	if
igloo	iglo
ignition	ign^n
ignorance	ignr^c
ignore	ignr
ill	il
illegal	ilgl
illicit	ilct
illness	ilns
illusion	il^n
illustrate	ilstrt
illustrated	ilstrtd
image	imj / img
imaginable	imgn^b/ imjn^b
imagination	imgn^n / imjn^n
imagine	imgn / imjn

imbalance	imbl^c
imitate	imtt
imitation	imt^n
immediate	imdit
immediately	imdit^y
immerse	imrs
immersion	imr^n
immigrant	imgrnt
immigration	imgr^n
imminent	imnnt
immovable	imv^b
immune	imn
immunity	imnty
immunization	imunz^n
immunize	imunz
impact	impct
impair	impr
impairment	impr^m
impartial	impr^s
impassable	imps^b
impatience	impa^c
impatient	imp^{n}t
impeccable	impc^b
impede	imped
impediment	impd^m
imperfect	imprfct
imperfection	imprfct^n
impermeable	imprma^b
implant	implnt
implausible	impls^b
implement	impl^m
implementation	impl^{mn}
implicating	implct^g
implication	implc^n
implore	implr
implored	implrd

imply	imp^y	inch	in$_c$
import	imprt	incidence	incd^c
importance	imprt^c	incident	incdnt
important	imprtnt / imp	incision	inc^n
importantly	imprtnt^y/imp^y	inclement	incl^m
importation	imprt^n	inclination	incln^n
impose	imps	incline	incln
imposition	imps^n	include	incld
impossible	imps^b	including	incld^g
impotence	impt^c	inclusion	incl^n
impotent	imptnt	incoherent	inchrnt
impress	im^{p}s	income	incm
impressed	im^{p}sd	incoming	incm^g
impression	im^{pn}	incompatible	in^{c}pt^b
impressive	im^{p}sv	incompetence	in^{c}pt^c
imprison	imprsn	incorporate	incrprt
imprisoned	imprsnd	increase	incrs
improbable	im^{p}b^b	increased	incrsd
improbably	im^{p}b^{by}	increasing	incrs^g
improvable	im^{p}v^b	increasingly	incrs^{gy}
improve	im^{p}v	incredible	incrd^b
improved	im^{p}vd	incredibly	incrd^{by}
improvement	im^{p}v^m	incubate	incubt
improvise	im^{p}vs	incubation	incub^n
imprudence	imprd^c	incurable	incr^b
impulse	impls	indecision	indcs^n
in	n	indeed	indd
in attendance	n-atnd^c	indefensible	indfns^b
inaccessible	inacs^b	indelible	indl^b
inactive	inctv	independence	indpnd^c
inadmissible	inadm^b	independent	indpndnt / indep
inadvisable	inadvs^b		
inaudible	inaud^b	index	indx
incapable	incp^b	indexation	indx^n
incarnation	incrn^n	Indian	indn / ind
incentive	insntv	indicate	indct

indicated	indctd	inflammable	$inflm^b$
indication	$indc^n$	inflatable	$inflt^b$
indicator	indctr	inflation	$infl^n$
indigenous	indgnos	inflexible	$inflx^b$
indigestion	$indgs^n$	influence	$influ^c$
indignation	$indgn^n$	influential	$influn^s$
indirect	indrct	inform	infrm
individual	indvl /indiv	informal	infrml
indolence	$indl^c$	information	$inform^n$ / info
indolent	indlnt	informed	infrmd
induce	indc	infrastructure	infrstrct
inducement	$indc^m$	infrequent	infrqnt
induction	$indc^n$	infringe	infrng / infrnj
indulge	indlg / indlj	infringement	$infrng^m$
indulgence	$indlg^c$	infuriate	infrit
industrial	indstrl	infuriation	$infri^n$
industry	$indst^y$	infuse	infus
inefficient	inefcnt	infusion	$infu^n$
ineligible	$inelg^b$	ingredient	ingrdnt
inertia	inrta	inhabit	inhbt
inescapable	$inescp^b$	inhabitable	$inhbt^b$
inevitable	$inevt^b$	inhabiting	$inhbt^g$
inevitably	$inevt^{by}$	inhale	inhl
inexcusable	$inxcs^b$	inhaling	$inhl^g$
inexorable	$inxr^b$	inherent	inhrnt
infallible	$infl^b$	inherit	inhrt
infant	infnt	inheritance	$inhrt^c$
infatuation	$inftu^n$	inherited	inhrtd
infect	infct	inhibit	inhbt
infection	$infc^n$	inhibition	$inhb^n$
infer	infr	in-house	n-hs
inference	$infr^c$	initial	in^s
infest	infst	initialing	in^{sg}
infestation	$infst^n$	initially	in^{sy}
infinite	infnt	initiate	intit
infinity	infnty / ∞	initiating	$intit^g$

initiation	inti^n	insistence	inst^c
initiative	intitv	inspect	inspct
inject	injct	inspection	inspc^n
injectable	injct^b	inspector	ispctr / insp
injection	injct^n	inspiration	inspr^n
injunction	injnc^n	inspire	inspr
injure	injr	install	instl
injuring	injr^g	installation	instl^n
injury	inj^y	installment	instl^m
inmate	inmt	instance	inst^c
inner	inr	instant	instnt
innocence	inc^c	instantly	instnt^y
innocent	incnt	instead	instd
innovation	inv^n	instigate	instgt
innovative	invtv	instigation	instg^n
innumerable	innmr^b	instill	instl
inoculate	inoclt	instinct	instnct
inoculating	inoclt^g	institution	instt^n
inoperable	inopr^b	institutional	instt^{nl}
inpatient	n-p^n_t	instruct	instrct
input	inpt	instruction	instrc^n
inquiry	inq^y	instructional	instrc^{nl}
inquisition	inqs^n	instructor	instrctr
inscribe	inscrb	instrument	instr^m
inscription	inscrp^n	insulate	inslt /inslat
insect	insct	insulating	inslt^g / inslat^g
insensible	insns^b	insulation	insl^n
inseparable	inspr^b	insulin	insln
insert	insrt	insult	inslt
insertion	insr^n	insulting	inslt^g
inside	insd	insurable	insr^b
insight	inst	insurance	insr^c
insightful	inst^f	insure	insr
insinuate	insnut	insurgence	insrg^c
insinuation	insnu^n	insurgency	insrg^{cy}
insist	inst	insurgent	insgnt

intact	intct	interdental	^{i}dntl
intangible	intng^b	interdepartmental	^{i}dpt^{ml}
integrate	intgrt	interdependence	dpnd^c
integrated	intgrtd	interdependent	^{i}dpndnt
integration	intgr^n	interdivisional	^{i}dv^{nl}
integrity	intgry	interest	^{i}st
intellectual	intlctl	interested	^{i}std
intelligence	intlg^c / intel	interesting	^{i}st^g
intelligent	intlgnt	interestingly	^{i}st^{gy}
intelligible	intlg^b	interests	^{i}sts
intend	intnd	interethnic	^{i}etnc
intended	intndd	interface	^{i}fc
intense	int^c	interfaith	^{i}ft
intensity	int^{c}ty	interfamily	^{i}fm^y
intent	intnt	interfere	^{i}fr
intention	intn^n	interfered	^{i}frd
intentionally	intn^{nly}	interference	^{i}fr^c
interact	^{i}act	intergeneration	^{i}gnr^n
interacted	^{i}actd	intergenerational	^{i}gnr^{nl}
interaction	^{i}ac^n	interim	^{i}m
interactive	^{i}actv	interior	^{i}ior
interbred	^{i}brd	interject	^{i}jct
interbreed	^{i}bred	interjected	^{i}jctd
intercede	^{i}ced	interjection	^{i}jct^n
intercept	^{i}cpt	interlace	^{i}lc
intercepted	^{i}cptd	interlaced	^{i}lcd
interchange	$^i{}_c$ng	interleave	^{i}lv
interchangeable	$^i{}_c$ng^b	interlink	^{i}lnk
intercom	^{i}c	interlock	^{i}lk
interconnect	^{ic}ct	interlocked	^{i}lkd
interconnection	^{ic}c^n	interlocutor	^{i}lcutr
intercontinental	^{ic}tntl	interlude	^{i}ld
intercourse	^{i}crs	intermarry	^{i}m^y
intercultural	^{i}cltrl	intermediary	^{i}mdi^y
interdenominational	^{i}dnmn^{nl}	intermediate	^{i}mdit
		interminable	^{i}mn^b

interminably	^{i}mn^{by}	intervention	^{i}vn^n
intermingle	^{i}mngl	interview	^{i}vw / ^{i}vu
intermission	^{i}m^n	interviewed	^{i}vwd
intermittent	^{i}mtnt	interviewee	^{i}vwe
intermittently	^{i}mtnt^y	interviewer	^{i}vwr
intermix	^{i}mx	interwove	^{i}wv
intern	^{i}n	interwoven	^{i}wvn
internal	^{i}nl	intestine	intstn
internalize	^{i}nliz	intimate	intmt
international	^{i}n^{nl}	into	into / in2
interned	^{i}nd	intolerable	intlr^b
internet	^{i}nt	intolerance	intlr^c
internship	^{i}n^p	intractable	^{ia}ct^b
interpersonal	^{i}prsnl	intranet	^{ia}nt
interplay	^{i}ply	intravenous	^{ia}vnos
interpret	^{i}prt	intrigue	intrg
interpretation	^{i}prt^n	introduce	^{i}dc
interpreted	^{i}prtd	introduces	^{i}dcs
interpreter	^{i}prtr	introduction	^{i}dc^n
interracial	^{i}r^s	introductory	^{i}dct^y
interregional	^{i}rgnl	introspection	^{i}spc^n
interregnum	^{i}rgnm	introvert	^{i}vrt
interrelate	^{i}rlt	intrude	intrd
interrelationship	^{i}rla^{np}	intrusion	intr^n
interrogate	^{i}rgt	intuition	intui^n
interrogation	^{i}rg^n	invade	invd
interrogator	^{i}rgtr	invalid	invld
interrupt	^{i}rpt	invaluable	invlu^b
interrupted	^{i}rptd	invariable	invr^b
interruption	^{i}rp^n	invasion	inv^n
intersect	^{i}sct	invent	invnt
intersection	^{i}sc^n	invention	invn^n
intersperse	^{i}sprs	inventory	invnt^y
intertwine	^{i}twn	invest	invst
interval	^{i}vl	investigate	invstgt
intervene	^{i}vn	investigation	invstgt^n

investigator	invstgtr	issue	isu
investment	invst^m	it	t
investor	invstr	it's / its	ts / its
invisible	invs^b	Italian	itln
invitation	invt^n	item	itm
invite	invt	iterate	itrat
invoice	invc	itinerary	itnr^y / intin
invoiced	invcd	itself	itslf
involve	invlv		
involved	invlvd		
involvement	invlv^m		
Iraqi	irq		
Ireland	irlnd / ir		
Irish	ir$_s$		
iron	irn		
ironically	irnc^y		
irony	irny		
irrelevance	irlv^c		
irrelevant	irlvnt		
irreparable	irpr^b		
irresistible	irsst^b		
irresponsible	irspns^b		
irreverence	irvr^c		
irreversible	irvrs^b		
irrigation	irg^n		
irritable	irt^b		
irritation	irt^n		
is	s		
Islam	islm		
Islamic	islmc		
island	ilnd		
isn't	snt / isnt		
isolate	islt		
isolated	isltd		
isolation	isl^n		
Israeli	isrli / is		

J

jacket	jkt
jaguar	jgr
jail	jl
January	ja
Japanese	jpns /jap
jar	jr
jargon	jrgn
jaw	jw
jazz	jz
jeans	jns
jeer	jer
jellyfish	j^yf_s
jet	jt
jettison	jtsn
Jew	jw
jewelry	jwl^y
Jewish	jw_s
job	jb
jobless	jbls
jog	jg
join	jn
joint	jnt
joke	jk
journal	jrnl
journalism	jrnlsm
journalist	jrnlst
journey	jrny
joy	jy
joyful	jy^f
joyriding	$jyrd^g$
jubilation	jbl^n
judge	jg / jj
judgment	jg^m / jj^m
judicial	jd^s
juice	jc
July	jl
jump	jmp
junction	jnc^n
June	jn
jungle	jngl
junior	jnr
jurisdiction	$jrsdc^n$
juror	jrr
jury	j^y
just	jst
justice	jstc
justifiable	$jstfi^b$
justify	jstfy

K

kangaroo	kngro /roo
keen	kn
keep	kp
kept	kpt
key	ky / ke
keyboard	kybrd
keynote	kynt
kick	kk
kid	kd
kidnap	kdnp
kidnapped	kdnpd
kidney	kdny
kill	kl
killer	klr
killing	kl^g
kind	knd
king	k^g
kingdom	k^{g}dm
kiss	ks
kit	kt
kitchen	k$_c$n
knead	ned
knee	ne
kneel	nel
knew	nw
knife	nf
knock	nk
know	no
knowledge	nolj / nolg
known	nwn
knows	nos

knuckle	nkl
koala	kla
Koran	krn
Korean	kren

L

lab	lb
label	lbl
labor	lbr
laboratory	lbrt^y / lab
labrador	lbrdr / lab
lacerate	lcrt / lsrt
laceration	lcrt^n
lack	lk
lactation	lct^n
ladder	ldr
lady	ldy
ladybird	ldybrd
lake	lk
lament	l^m
laminate	lmnt
lamination	lmn^n
lamp	lmp
land	lnd
landfill	lndfl
landing	lnd^g
landlord	lndlrd
landmark	lndmrk
landowner	lndonr
landowning	lndon^g
landscape	lndscp

lane	ln	leaf	lf
language	lngj/lngg/lang	leaflet	lflt
languish	lngi$_s$	league	lg
lap	lp	leak	lk
large	lrg / L	lean	ln
largely	lrg^y	leap	lp
laser	lsr	learn	lrn
last	lst	learning	lrn^g
lasted	lstd	lease	les
latch	l$_c$	least	lst / lest
late	lt	leather	l$_t$r
lately	lt^y	leave	lv
later	ltr / latr	leaver	lvr
lateral	ltrl	lecture	lctr
Latin	ltn	lecturer	lctrr
latter	ltr	led	ld
laugh	lgh / lf	left	lft
laughable	lgh^b / lf^b	leftwing	lftw^g
laughter	lghtr / lftr	leg	lg
launch	ln$_c$	legacy	lgcy
lavish	lv$_s$	legal	lgl
lavished	lv$_s$d	legalize	lgliz
law	lw	legally	lg^y
lawbreaker	lwbrkr	legend	lgnd
lawbreaking	lwbrk^g	legible	lg^b
lawful	lw^f	legislate	lgslt
lawmaker	lwmkr	legislation	lgsl^n
lawn	lwn	legislative	lgsltv
lawsuit	lwst	legislator	lgsltr
lawyer	lwyr	legislature	lgsltur
lay	ly	legitimate	legtmt
layer	lyr	lemon	lmn
lead	ld	lend	lnd
leader	ldr	length	lng$_t$
leadership	ldr^p	lenience	lni^c
leading	ld^g	lenient	lnint

lens	lns	lightning	ltn^g
lesion	l^n	likable	lk^b
less	ls / <	like	lk
less than	<	likelihood	lklhd
lessen	lsn	likely	lk^y
lesser	lsr	liken	lkn
lesson	lsn / lson	likewise	lkws
let	lt	lilac	llc
letter	ltr	limb	lmb
level	lvl	limit	lmt
leverage	lvrj / lvrg	limitation	lmt^n
levied	lvd	limited	lmtd / ltd
levitate	lvtt	line	ln / lin
levy	lvy	link	lnk
liability	li^{bty}	lion	ln / lin
liable	li^b	lip	lp
liaise	lias	liquid	lqd
libel	lbl	list	lst
liberal	lbrl	listen	lstn
liberate	lbrt	listener	lstnr
liberation	lbr^n	listening	$lstn^g$
liberty	lbrty	literally	ltry / $ltrl^y$
library	lbr^y	literary	ltr^y
license	lc^c	literature	ltrtr / lit
licensing	lc^{cg}	litigate	ltgt
lid	ld	litigation	ltg^n
lie	li	litter	ltr
life	lf	little	ltl
lifestyle	lfstl	live	lv
lifetime	lftm	liver	lvr
lift	lft	living	lv^g
ligament	lg^m	lizard	lzd
ligature	lgtr	load	ld
light	lt	loaded	ldd
lighting	lt^g	loan	ln
lightly	lt^y	lobby	lby

local	lcl
locality	lclty
localize	lcliz
locate	lcat
location	lc^n
lock	lk
locked	lkd
lodge	lj / lg
lodged	ljd / lgd
loft	lft
log	lg
logic	lgc
logical	lgcl
loin	ln / lon
loiter	ltr
lone	ln / lon
lonely	ln^y
long	lng
long-term	lng-trm
longtime	lngtm
look	lk
loop	lp
loophole	lphl
loose	ls / los
loosen	lsn
looter	ltr
looting	lt^g
lose	ls / los
loss	ls
lost	lst
lot	lt
lotion	l^n
lots	lts
loud	ld
lounge	lng / lnj
lovable	lv^b

love	lv
lovely	lv^y
lover	lvr
low	lw / lo
lower	lwr
loyal	lyl
loyalty	lylty
lubricate	lbrct
lubrication	$lbrc^n$
luck	lk
lucky	lky
lucrative	lcrtv
lunch	ln_c
lung	lng
lush	l_s
lust	lst
lustful	lst^f
lying	ly^g

M

machine	m$_c$n
mad	md
maddening	mdn^g
made	md
magazine	mgzn / mag
magic	mgc
magnate	mgnt
magnet	mgnt
magnetic	mgntc
magnify	mgnfy
magnitude	mgntd
magpie	mgpi
mail	ml
main	mn
mainly	mn^y
mainstream	mnstrm
maintain	mntn
maintenance	mntn^c
major	mjr
majority	mjrty
make	mk
makeover	mk^o
maker	mkr
makeup	mkup
male	ml/ M / ♂
malfunction	mlfnc^n
malignancy	mlgn^{cy}
malignant	mlgnnt
malinger	mlngr
mall	ml
maltreat	mltrt
mammal	mml
mammoth	mm$_t$
man	mn
manage	mng / mnj
manageable	mng^b
management	mng^m
manager	mngr
managing	mng^g
mandate	mndt
mandatory	mndt^y
maneuver	mnvr
maneuvered	mnvrd
manhandle	mnhndl
manhandled	mnhndld
manifest	mnfst
manipulate	mnplt
manner	mnr
mansion	mn^n
manufacture	mnfctr/manu
manufacturer	mnfctrr
manufacturing	mnfctr^g
many	mny
map	mp
maple	mpl
mapped	mpd
marble	mrbl
march	mr$_c$
March	ma
margin	mrgn
marginal	mrgnl
marine	mrn
mark	mrk
marked	mrkd
marker	mrkr
market	mrkt / mkt
marketable	mrkt^b

marketing	$mrkt^g$	meaning	mn^g
marketplace	mktplc	meaningful	mn^{gf}
maroon	mron	meant	mnt
marriage	mrg / mrj	meantime	mntm
married	mrd	meanwhile	$mn_w l$
marrow	mrw	measurable	msr^b
marry	m^y	measure	msr
marshal	$mr_s l$	measurement	msr^m
marvel	mrvl	meat	mt
mash	m_s	mechanic	$m_c nc$ / mech
mask	msk	mechanical	$m_c ncl$
mass	ms	mechanism	$m_c nsm$
massage	msj / msg	medal	mdl
massive	msv	media	mda
master	mstr	mediate	mdit
match	m_c	mediation	mdi^n
matchbox	$m_c bx$	medical	mdcl
mate	mt	medicate	mdct
material	mtrl / mtril	medication	mdc^n
maternity	mtrnty / mat	medicine	mdcn
math	m_t	mediocre	mdocr
mathematics	m_t mtcs/math	meditate	mdtt
matter	mtr	meditation	mdt^n
mature	mtur	medium	mdm /med
matured	mturd	meet	mt
maturely	$mtur^y$	meeting	mt^g
maximize	mxmiz	melody	mldy
maximum	mxm / max	melt	mlt
May	my	member	mbr
may	ma / my	members	mbrs
maybe	myb	membership	mbr^p
mayor	myr	membrane	mbrn
me	m	memo	mo
meal	ml	memorable	mr^b / mem^b
mean	mn	memorandum	mo / memo
meander	mendr		

memorized	mrzd / memd	mild	mld
memory	m^y / mem	mile	ml
men	mn	milestone	mlstn
mend	mnd	militant	mltnt
menial	mnil	military	mlt^y
mental	mntl	milk	mlk
mentally	mnt^y	mill	ml
mention	mn^n	million	mln / 10^6
mentioned	mn^{nd}	millionaire	mlnar
mentor	mntr	mind	mnd
mentored	mntrd	mindset	mndst
menu	mnu	mine	mn / min
merchandise	mr_cnds	mineral	mnrl
merchant	mr_cnt	mingle	mngl
mere	mr	minimal	mnml
merely	mr^y	minimize	mnmiz
merge	mrg	minimum	mnm / min
merit	mrt	minister	mnstr
mess	ms	ministry	$mnst^y$
message	msg / msj	minor	mnr
metal	mtl	minority	mnrty
metaphor	mtfr	minute	mnt / mn
meter	mtr	minutes	mnts / mns
method	m_td	minute-taker	mnt-tkr m/t
methodology	m_td^o	miracle	mrcl
metropolitan	mtrpltn/metro	mirror	mrr
Mexican	mxcn /mx	misadvise	msadvs
microbiology	mcrbi^o	misalign	msalgn
microscope	mcrscp	misbehave	msbhv
microwave	mcrwv	miscellaneous	mclnos/misc
middle	mdl / mid	misconduct	ms^{c}dct
midnight	mdnt	miscounted	mscntd
midst	mdst	misdirect	msdrct
midwife	mdwf	miserable	msr^b
might	mt	misgiving	msgv^g
migration	mgr^n	misguided	msgdd

mishandle	mshndl	mole	ml / mol
mislead	msled	molecular	mlclr
misled	msld	molecule	mlcl
mismatch	msm_c	molest	mlst
misplace	msplc	mom	m
misquote	msqt	moment	m^m
miss	ms	momentum	$m^m m$
missed	msd	Monday	mo
missile	msl	money	mny
missing	ms^g	moneymaking	$mnymk^g$
mission	m^n	mongrel	mngrl
missionary	m^{ny}	monitor	mntr
mistake	mstk	monkey	mnky
mistaken	mstkn	monster	mnstr
mistreat	mstrt	month	mn_t
mistrust	mstrst	monthly	mn_t^y
mitigate	mtgt	monument	mnu^m
mitigation	mtg^n	mood	md
mix	mx	moon	mn / mon
mixed	mxd	moose	ms /mos
mixture	mxtr	moral	mrl
mm-hmm	m-hm	more	mr
moan	mon	moreover	mr^o
mobile	mbl / mob	moribund	mribnd
mode	md /mod	morning	mrn^g
model	mdl	mortality	mrtlty
modeled	mdld	mortgage	mrgg/ mrgj/ mrg
modem	mdm	most	mst
moderate	mdrt	mostly	mst^y
moderation	mdr^n	moth	m_t
moderator	mdrtr	mothballed	$m_t bld$
modern	mdrn	mother	$m_t r$
modernize	mdrniz	motion	m^n
modest	mdst	motivate	mtvt
modification	$mdfc^n$		
modify	mdfy		

motivation	mtv^n	multiscreen	^{m}scrn
motive	mtv	multisensory	^{m}sns^y
motor	mtr	multistory	^{m}st^y
motorized	mtrzd	multitalented	^{m}tlntd
mount	mnt	multitasking	^{m}tsk^g
mountain	mntn / mt	multivitamins	^{m}vtmns/^{m}vits
mouse	mos	mumble	mbl
mouth	m$_t$	municipal	mncpl
move	mv	murder	mrdr
movement	mv^m	murdered	mrdrd
movie	mve	murmur	mrmr
Mr	mr	muscle	msl
Mrs	mrs	museum	msm
Ms	ms	mushroom	m$_s$rm
much	m$_c$	music	msc
mucus	mucs	musical	mscl
mud	md	musician	ms^n
muddy	mdy	Muslim	mslm
mule	ml /mul	must	mst
multicolor	^{m}clr	mutate	mutt
multicolored	^{m}clrd	mute	mut
multicultural	^{m}cltrl	mutter	mtr
multidisciplinary	^{md}pln^y	mutual	mtl
multifunction	^{m}fnc^n	my	my
multifunctional	^{m}fnc^{nl}	myself	myslf
multilateral	^{m}ltrl	mysterious	mstros
multi-lingual	^{m}lngl	mystery	mst^y
multimedia	^{m}mda	myth	m$_t$
multimillion	^{m}mln		
multipack	^{m}pk		
multiplayer	^{m}plyr		
multiple	^{m}pl		
multiplication	^{m}plc^n		
multiply	^{m}p^y		
multipurpose	^{m}prps		
multiracial	^{m}r^s		

N

nag	ng
nail	nl
naked	nkd
name	nm
named	nmd
narcotic	nrctc
narrate	nrt
narrative	nrtv
narrator	nrtr
narrow	nrw / nro
nasal	nsl
nasty	nsty
natal	ntl
nation	n^n
national	n^{nl}
nationwide	n^nwd
native	ntv
natural	ntrl
naturally	ntr^y
nature	ntr
nausea	nsa
nauseating	nsat^g
navigable	nvg^b
navigate	nvgt
navigation	nvg^n
navigational	nvg^{nl}
Neanderthal	nndr$_t$l
near	nr
nearby	nrby
nearly	nr^y
neat	nt
nebulizer	nbulzr / neb
necessarily	ncsr^y
necessary	ncs^y
necessity	ncsty
neck	nk
need	nd
needle	ndl
negate	ngat
negative	ngtv / -
neglect	nglct
neglectful	nglct^f
negligence	nglg^c
negligible	nglg^b
negotiable	ngot^b
negotiate	ngott
negotiation	ngot^n
neighbor	nbr
neighborhood	nbrhd
neighboring	nbrg
neither	n$_t$r
neonatal	nontl /neo
nerve	nrv
nervous	nrvos
nest	nst
net	nt
network	ntwrk
neural	nrl
neutral	ntrl
never	nvr
nevertheless	nvr$_t$ls
new	nw
newly	nw^y
news	nws
newspaper	nwspr
next	nxt
nice	nc

nicotine	nctin	nose	ns
niggle	ngl	not	nt
night	nt	note	nt / nb
nightmare	ntmr	notebook	ntbk
nine	9	noted	ntd
nineteen	19	note-taker	ntkr
ninth	9th / 9_t	nothing	$n_t g$ / 0
nip	np	notice	ntc
nipple	npl	noticeable	ntc^b
nitpicking	$ntpk^g$	notified	ntfyd
no	no / x	notify	ntfy
nobody	nbdy	notion	n^n
nod	nd	notional	n^{nl}
noise	nos	noun	nn / non
nominate	nmnt	nourish	nr_s
nomination	nmn^n	nourishing	$nr_s g$
nominee	nmne	nourishment	$nr_s m$
nonchalance	$nn_c l^c$	novel	nvl
nonchalant	$nn_c lnt$	now	nw
none	nn	nowhere	$n_w r$
nonetheless	$nn_t ls$	nuance	nu^c
non-executive	nn-xctv/ nxec	nuclear	nclr
non-payer	nnpyr	nuisance	nus^c
non-paying	$nnpy^g$	nullify	nlfy
nonprofit	nnprft	numb	nm
non-voting	$nnvt^g$	number	no / nmbr
noon	nn / 12	numeral	nmrl
nor	nr	numerous	nmros
norm	nrm	nuptial	np^s
normal	nrml	nurse	nrs
normalize	nrmlz	nut	nt
normally	nrm^y	nutrient	ntrnt
north	nr_t / n	nutrition	ntr^n
northeast	ne	nutritional	ntr^{nl}
northern	$nr_t n$	nutritious	ntrtos
northwest	nw		

O

o'clock	oclk
oak	ok
oath	o$_t$
obedience	obd^c
obedient	obdnt
obese	obs
obey	oby
object	objct
objection	objct^n
objective	objctv / obj
obligation	oblg^n
oblige	oblg / oblj
obscure	obscr
obscured	obscrd
observation	obsrv^n
observe	obsrv
observer	obsrvr
obsess	obss
obsession	obs^n
obsessive	obssv
obsolete	obslt
obstacle	obstcl
obstruct	obstrct
obstruction	obstrc^n
obtain	obtn
obtainable	obtn^b
obvious	obvos
obviously	obvos^y
occasion	oca^n
occasional	oca^{nl}
occasionally	oca^{ny}

occupation	ocp^n / occ
occupy	ocpy
occur	ocr
occurrence	ocr^c
ocean	o^n
October	oc
octopus	octps
odd	od
odds	ods
of	f
off	of
offence	of^c
offend	ofnd
offender	ofndr
offense	of^c
offensive	of^{c}v
offer	ofr
offered	ofrd
offering	ofr^g
office	ofc
officer	ofcr
official	of^s
officially	of^{sy}
offload	ofld
offloaded	ofldd
offset	ofst
offspring	ofspr^g
often	oftn / oft
oh	o
oil	ol
ok	ok / k
okay	ok / k
old	old
old-fashioned	old-f$_s$nd
Olympic	olpc
Olympics	olpcs

omission	omi^n	optimal	optml
omit	omt	optimistic	optmstc
on	on / o / n	optimized	optmzd
once	o^c	option	op^n
oncologist	onclgst	optional	op^{nl}
oncology	onc^o	options	op^{n}s
one	1	or	or
one-half	1/2	oral	orl
one-quarter	1/4	orally	or^y
one-third	1/3	orangutan	orngtn
ongoing	ong^g	orange	orng
onion	onn	orbit	orbt
online	onln	ordain	ordn
onlooker	onlkr	order	ordr
only	on^y	ordinary	ordn^y /ordin
onto	on2	organ	orgn
open	opn	organic	orgnc
opening	opn^g	organism	orgnsm
openly	opn^y	organization	orgnz^n
opera	opra	organizational	orgnz^{nl}
operable	opr^b	organize	orgniz
operate	oprt	organized	orgnzd
operating	oprt^g	orientating	orintt^g
operation	opr^n / op	orientation	orint^n
operator	oprtr	orienting	orint^g
opinion	opnn / opn	origin	orgn
opponent	opnt	original	orgnl
opportunity	oprtnty / opp	originally	orgn^y
oppose	ops	origination	orgn^n
opposed	opsd	ornament	orn^m
opposite	opst	orthopedic	or$_t$pdc / or$_t$o
opposition	opos^n	ostrich	ostr$_c$
oppressed	oprsd	other	o$_t$r
oppression	oprs^n	others	o$_t$rs
opt	opt	otherwise	o$_t$rws
opted	optd	otter	otr

ought	ot	oven	ovn
our	r	over	^{o}
ours	rs	overachieve	$^{o}a_{c}v$
ourselves	rslvs	overact	^{o}act
oust	ost	overall	^{o}al
out	ot	overarching	$^{o}ar_{c}{}^{g}$
outbid	otbd	overbalance	$^{o}bl^{c}$
outclass	otcls	overbearing	$^{o}br^{g}$
outclassed	otclsd	overcautious	$^{o}ctos$
outcome	otcm	overcome	^{o}cm
outdated	otdtd	overdo	^{o}do
outdistance	otdst^{c}	overdose	^{o}ds
outdo	otdo	overdraft	$^{o}drft$
outdoing	otd^{g}	overdue	^{o}du
outdoor	otdr	overflow	^{o}flw
outer	otr	overfunding	$^{o}fnd^{g}$
outfit	outft	overgrow	^{o}grw
outgoing	otg^{g}	overhang	^{o}hng
outgrow	otgro	overhear	^{o}hr
outlast	otlst	overhype	^{o}hp
outlawed	otlwd	overlap	^{o}lp
outlet	otlt	overlay	^{o}ly
outline	otln	overload	^{o}ld
outlined	otlnd	overlook	^{o}lk
outlived	otlvd	overnight	^{o}nt
outplacement	otplc^{m}	overpay	^{o}py
outpouring	otpr^{g}	overpayment	$^{o}py^{m}$
output	otpt	overreact	^{o}act
outreach	otr$_{c}$	overreaction	$^{o}ac^{n}$
outsell	otsl	override	^{o}id
outside	otsd	overrule	^{o}ul
outsider	otsdr	oversee	^{o}se / ^{o}c
outsource	otsrc	overshadow	$^{o}{}_{s}dw$
outstanding	otstnd^{g}	oversight	^{o}st
outwit	owt	overstate	^{o}stt
outwith	otw$_{t}$	overstay	^{o}sty

overtake	^{o}tk
overtrade	^{o}trd
overview	^{o}vw / ^{o}vu
overweight	^{o}wt
overwhelm	^o_wlm
overwhelming	^o_wlm^g
overworked	^{o}wrkd
overwritten	^{o}rtn
ovulation	ovul^n
owe	ow
owl	ol /owl
own	own
owner	ownr
ownership	ownr^p
oxygen	O_2 / ox / oxy
oyster	ostr

P

pace	pc
pacemaker	pcmkr
pacify	pcfy
pack	pk
package	pkg / pkj
pact	pct
pad	pd
page	pg / pj
pain	pn
painful	pn^f
painkiller	pnklr
paint	pnt
painter	pntr
painting	pnt^g
pair	pr
palace	plc
pale	pl
Palestinian	plstnn
palm	plm
palpitation	plpt^n
pamper	pmpr
pan	pn
panda	pnda
panel	pnl
panic	pnc
pant	pnt
paper	ppr
parade	prd
paragraph	prgrf / para
parallel	prll
paralyze	prlyz

paramedic	prmdc	patent	ptnt
parameter	prmtr	path	p_t
parcel	prcl	pathology	$p_t{}^o$
parent	prnt	patience	ps^c
parental	prntl	patient	psnt
parish	pr_s	patrol	ptrl
parity	prty	patron	ptrn
park	prk	patronage	ptrnj / ptrng
parking	prk^g	patronize	ptrniz
parliament	$prli^m$	pattern	ptrn
part	prt	pause	ps
partial	pr^s	pavement	pv^m
partially	pr^{sy}	pawn	pwn
participant	prtcpnt	pay	py / pa
participate	prtcpt	payable	py^b / pa^b
participation	$prtcp^n$	payback	pybk / pabk
particle	prtcl	payment	py^m / pa^m
particular	prtclr / part	PC	pc
particularly	$prtclr^y$	peace	pec / pes
partition	prt^n	peaceful	pec^f
partly	prt^y	peach	p_c
partner	prtnr	peak	pk
partnership	$prtnr^p$	peanut	pnt
party	prty	peasant	psnt
pass	ps	pediatric	pdtrc / ped
passable	ps^b	peel	pl
passage	psg /psj	peer	pr
passenger	psgr /psjr	pen	pn
passing	ps^g	penalty	pnlty
passion	p^n	pence	p^c
past	pst	pencil	pncl
pasta	psta	pending	pnd^g
paste	past	penetrate	pntrt
pastor	pstr	penetration	$pntr^n$
pat	pt	penguin	pngn
patch	p_c		

pension	pn^n	personal	^psnl
pensionable	pn^{nb}	personality	^psnlty
people	ppl	personally	$^psn^y$
pepper	ppr	personnel	^psnel
per	^{p}	perspective	^pspctv
perceive	^pcv	perspiration	$^pspr^n$
perceived	^pcvd	persuade	^psad
percentage	^pcntg / %	persuasion	$^psa^n$
perceptible	$^pcpt^b$	perverse	^pvrs
perception	$^pcp^n$	perversely	$^pvrs^y$
perfect	^pfct	perversion	$^pvr^n$
perfection	$^pfct^n$	pervert	^pvrt
perfectly	$^pfct^y$	pester	pstr
perforate	^pfrt	pet	pt
perforation	$^pfr^n$	petition	pt^n
perform	^pfrm	pharmacy	phrmcy / frmcy/ pharm
performance	$^pfrm^c$	phase	phs / fs
performer	^pfrmr	phenomenon	phnmnn / fnmnn
perhaps	^phps	philosophical	phlosfcl / flosfcl
period	^pid	philosophy	ph^o / f^o
peripheral	^pfrl	phone	phn / fn
perish	$^p{}_s$	phony	phny / fny
perjury	pj^y	photo	phto / fto
perk	^pk	photograph	phtogrph / ftogrf /photo
permanent	^pmnnt	photographer	phtogrphr / ftogrfr
permeate	^pmat	photography	phtogrphy / ftogrfy
permission	$^pm^n$	phrase	phrs / frs
permit	^pmt	physical	phscl / fscl
persecute	^pscut	physically	$phsc^y$ / fsc^y
persecution	$^pscu^n$	physician	phs^n / fs^n
persevere	^psver		
Persian	p^n		
persist	^psst		
persistence	$^psst^c$		
person	^psn		

physics	phscs / fscs	pizza	pza
physiology	phsi^o / fsi^o	place	plc
physiotherapy	phsio$_t$rpy /	placement	plc^m
	fsio$_t$rpy/physio	plain	plan
piano	pno	plan	pln
pick	pk	plane	plan
picked	pkd	planet	plnt / plnet
picketing	pkt^g	planned	plnd
pickup	pkup	planner	plnr
picture	pctr / pic	planning	pln^g
pie	pi	plant	plnt
piece	pes	plastic	plstc
pierce	pierc	plate	plt
pig	pg	plateau	pltu
pigeonhole	pjnhl	platform	pltfrm
pigment	pg^m	plausible	pls^b
pile	pl /pil	play	ply
pilfer	plfr	player	plyr
pill	pl	playoff	plyof
pillow	plw / plo	plea	ple
pilot	plt	plead	pld
pin	pn	pleasant	plsnt
pinch	pn$_c$	please	pls
pine	pn / pin	pleased	plsd
pink	pnk	pleasurable	plsr^b
pinpoint	pnpnt	pleasure	plsr
pioneer	pionr	pledge	plj / plg
pip	pp	plentiful	plnt^f
pipe	pp /pip	plenty	plnty
pipeline	ppln	pliable	pli^b
pit	pt	plot	plt
pitch	p$_c$	plug	plg
pitcher	p$_c$r	plumber	plmr
pitiful	pt^f	plumbing	plm^g
pittance	pt^c	plummet	plmt
pivot	pvt	plunge	plng

plural	plrl	population	ppl^n
plus	+	porch	pr_c
PM	pm	pork	prk
poach	po_c	port	prt
pocket	pkt	portable	prt^b
poem	pm / pom	portfolio	prtflo
poet	pot	portion	pr^n
poetry	ptry	portrait	prtrt
point	pnt	portray	prtry
pointed	pntd	pose	ps
poison	posn	position	ps^n
poisoned	posnd	positive	pstv / +
poke	pk	possess	pss
pole	pl	possession	ps^n
police	plc	possibility	ps^{bty} / pos
policeman	plcmn	possible	ps^b
policewoman	plcwmn	possibly	ps^{by}
policy	plcy	post	pst
Polish	pl_s	postdated	pstdtd
polish	pl_s	poster	pstr
political	pltcl	postmarked	pstmrkd
politically	$pltc^y$	postnatal	pstntl
politician	plt^n	postpone	pstpn
politics	pltcs	pot	pt
poll	pl	potato	pto
pollinate	plnat	potential	ptn^s
pollute	plut	potentially	ptn^{sy}
pollution	pl^n	pound	pnd / £ / lb
pond	pnd	pour	pr
ponder	pndr	poverty	pvrty
pool	pl / pol	powder	pwdr
poor	pr / por	power	pwr
pop	pp	powered	pwrd
popular	pplr	powerful	pwr^f
popularity	pplrty	practicable	$prctc^b$
populate	pplt	practical	prctcl

practically	$prctc^y$	preconceive	$^pc cv$
practice	prctc	preconceived	$^pc cvd$
practitioner	$prct^n r$	precondition	$^pc d^n$
praise	prs	predate	$^p dt$
pray	pry	predator	$^p dtr$
prayer	pryr	predatory	$^p dt^y$
pre admission	$^p adm^n$	predecease	$^p dces$
pre adult	$^p adlt$	predestined	$^p dstnd$
pre approve	$^p aprv$	predicament	$^p dc^m$
pre book	$^p bk$	predict	$^p dct$
pre check	$^p ck$	predictable	$^p dct^b$
pre order	$^p ord$	predictably	$^p dct^{by}$
pre treat	$^p trt$	predicted	$^p dctd$
preach	$^p{}_c$	prediction	$^p dc^n$
preacher	$^p{}_c r$	predisposed	$^{pd} psd$
preamble	$^p ambl$	predominance	$^p dmn^c$
prearrange	$^p arng$	predominant	$^p dmnnt$
prearranged	$^p arngd$	preeminent	$^p emnnt$
precancerous	$^p cncros$	preempt	$^p empt$
precarious	$^p cros$	preexist	$^p xst$
precariously	$^p cros^y$	preexistence	$^p xst^c$
precaution	$^p c^n$	prefabricate	$^p fbrct$
precautionary	$^p c^{ny}$	preface	$^p fc$
precede	$^p ced$	prefect	$^p fct$
preceded	$^p cedd$	prefer	$^p fr$
precedence	$^p cd^c$	preferable	$^p fr^b$
precedent	$^p cdnt$	preferably	$^p fr^{by}$
precinct	$^p cnct$	preference	$^p fr^c$
precious	$^p cos$	preferential	$^p frn^s$
precipitate	$^p cptt$	preferred	$^p frd$
precipitated	$^p cpttd$	prefix	$^p fx$
precise	$^p cs$	pregnancy	$prgn^{cy}$
precisely	$^p cs^y$	pregnant	$^p gnnt$ / preg
precision	$^p c^n$	prehistoric	$^p hstrc$
preclude	$^p cld$	prejudge	$^p jg$ / $^p jj$
precocious	$^p ccos$	prejudice	$^p jdc$

Word	Shorthand	Word	Shorthand
prejudicial	pjds	presidency	psdcy
preliminary	plmny	president	psdnt / pres
premature	pmtr	presidential	psdns
prematurely	pmtry	press	ps
premier	pmir	pressure	p$_s$r
premiership	pmirp	pressured	p$_s$rd
premise	pms	prestige	pstg
premium	pmum	presumably	psmby
premonition	pmnn	presume	psm
preoccupied	pocpd	presumed	psmd
preparation	ppran	presumption	psmpn
prepare	ppr	presuppose	psps
prepared	pprd	presupposition	pspsn
prepay	ppy	pretend	ptnd
prepayment	ppym	pretended	ptndd
preplanned	pplnd	pretense	ptc
preponderance	ppndrc	pretentious	ptntos
preregister	prgstr	pretty	pty / prty
prescribe	pscrb	prevail	pvl
prescription	pscrpn	prevailed	pvld
prescriptive	pscrptv	prevalence	pvlc
preselect	pslct	prevalent	pvlnt
presence	psc	prevaricate	pvrct
present	psnt	prevent	pvnt
presentable	psntb	preventable	pvntb
presentably	psntby	preventative	pvnttv
presentation	psntn	prevention	pvnn
presented	psntd	preview	pvw / pvu
presenter	psntr	previous	pvos
presently	psnty	previously	pvosy
preservation	psrvn	prewarm	pwrm
preserve	psrv	prey	py / pry
preserved	psrvd	price	prc
preset	pst	priceless	prcls
preside	psd	prick	prk
presided	psdd	pride	prd

priest	prst	probation	$^{p}b^{n}$
priggish	prg_{s}	probe	^{p}rb
primacy	prmcy	probed	^{p}rbd
primal	prml	problem	^{p}blm
primarily	$prmr^{y}$	problematic	$^{p}blmtc$
primary	prm^{y}	procedural	$^{p}cdrl$
prime	prm	procedure	^{p}cdr
primitive	prmtv	proceed	^{p}cd
principal	prncpl	proceeded	^{p}cdd
principle	prncpl	proceeds	^{p}cds
principled	prncpld	process	^{p}cs
principles	prncpls	processes	^{p}css
print	prnt	processing	$^{p}cs^{g}$
printable	$prnt^{b}$	procession	$^{p}s^{n}$
printer	prntr	processor	^{p}ssr
printout	prntot	proclaim	^{p}clm
prior	pror	procrastinate	$^{p}crstnt$
priorities	prorts	procrastination	$^{p}crstn^{n}$
prioritize	prortz	procure	^{p}cr
priority	prorty	procurement	$^{p}cr^{m}$
prison	prsn	prodigy	^{p}dgy
prisoner	prsnr	produce	^{p}dc
privacy	prvcy	produced	^{p}dcd
private	prvt	producer	^{p}dcr
privately	$prvt^{y}$	produces	^{p}dcs
privation	$prva^{n}$	product	^{p}dct
privatize	prvtiz	production	$^{p}dc^{n}$
privatized	prvtzd	productive	$^{p}dctv$
privilege	prvlg / prvlj	productivity	$^{p}dctvty$
privileged	prvlgd	profanity	$^{p}fnty$
prize	prz	profess	^{p}fs
pro	p	profession	$^{p}fs^{n}$
proactive	$^{p}actv$	professional	$^{p}fs^{nl}$
probability	$^{p}b^{bty}$	professionally	$^{p}fs^{nly}$
probable	$^{p}b^{b}$	professor	^{p}fsr
probably	$^{p}b^{by}$	proffer	^{p}fr

proficiency	$^pf^ncy$	promotion	$^pm^n$
proficient	$^pf^nt$	promotional	$^pm^{nl}$
profile	^pfl	prompt	^pmpt
profit	^pft	promptly	$^pmpt^y$
profitability	$^pft^{bty}$	prone	^pn
profitable	$^pft^b$	pronounce	$^pn^c$
profligate	^pflgt	pronounced	$^pn^cd$
profound	^pfnd	pronouncement	$^pn^{cm}$
profuse	^pfs	pronunciation	$^pnca^n$
prognosis	^pgnss	proof	^pf
program	^pgrm	proofread	^pfrd
programmed	^pgrmd	propaganda	^ppgnda
programmer	^pgrmr	propagate	^ppgt
programming	$^pgrm^g$	propel	^ppl
progress	^pgrs	proper	^ppr
progression	$^pgr^n$	properly	$^ppr^y$
progressive	^pgrsv	property	^pprty
progressively	$^pgrsv^y$	prophesy	^pfsy
prohibit	^phbt	prophetic	^pftc
prohibition	$^phb^n$	proponent	^ppnnt
prohibitive	^phbtv	proportion	$^pp^n$
project	^pjct	proportional	$^pp^{nl}$
projected	^pjctd	proportionality	$^pp^nlty$
projection	$^pjc^n$	proportionally	$^pp^{nly}$
projector	^pjctr	proportionate	$^pp^nt$
proliferate	^plfrt	proportions	$^ppr^ns$
proliferation	$^plfr^n$	proposal	^ppsl
prolific	^plfc	propose	^pps
prominence	$^pmn^c$	proposed	^ppsd
prominent	^pmnnt	proposer	^ppsr
prominently	$^pmnnt^y$	proposition	$^pps^n$
promiscuity	^pmscuty	proprietor	^pprtr
promiscuous	^pmscus	prosaic	^psc
promise	^pms	prosecute	^psct
promising	$^pms^g$	prosecution	$^psc^n$
promote	^pmt	prosecutor	^psctr

prospect	^{P}spct	provided	^{P}vidd
prospective	^{P}spctv	providence	^{P}vd^c
prospects	^{P}spcts	provider	^{P}vdr
prospectus	^{P}spctus	province	^{P}v^c
prosper	^{P}spr	provincial	^{P}vn^s
prosperous	^{P}spros	provision	^{P}v^n
prostate	^{P}stt	provisional	^{P}v^{nl}
prosthetic	^{P}s$_t$tc	proviso	^{P}vso
prostitute	^{P}sttut	provocation	^{P}vc^n
prostrate	^{P}trt	provocative	^{P}vctv
protect	^{P}tct	provoke	^{P}vk
protected	^{P}tctd	provoked	^{P}vkd
protection	^{P}tc^n	prowl	^{P}wl
protective	^{P}tctv	proximity	^{P}xmty
protectively	^{P}tctv^y	proxy	^{P}xy
protein	^{P}ten	prudence	prd^c
protest	^{P}tst	prudent	prdnt
protestant	^{P}tstnt	psychiatrist	sciatrst
protester	^{P}tstr	psychological	sclgcl
protocol	^{P}tcl	psychologist	sclgst
prototype	^{P}ttyp	psychology	psyc^o / sc^o
protract	^{P}trct	puberty	pbrty
protracted	^{P}trctd	public	pblc
protrude	^{P}trud	publication	pblc^n
protruded	^{P}trudd	publicity	pblcty
protrusion	^{P}tru^n	publicly	pblc^y
protuberance	^{P}tbr^c	publish	pbl$_s$
proud	^{P}d	publisher	pbl$_s$r
proudly	^{P}d^y	publishing	pbl$_s$g
prove	^{P}rv	pull	pl
proved	^{P}rvd	pulmonary	plmn^y
proven	^{P}vn	pulse	pls
provenance	^{P}vn^c	pump	pmp
proverb	^{P}vrb	punch	pn$_c$
proverbial	^{P}vbl	punctual	pnctl
provide	^{P}vid	punctuation	pncta^n

punish	pn_s	quest	qst
punishable	$pn_s b$	question	?
punishment	$pn_s m$	questionable	?b
pupil	ppl	questioning	?g
purchase	$pr_c s$	questionnaire	?ar
pure	pr /pur	queue	q
purple	prpl	quick	qk
purpose	prps	quicken	qkn
purse	prs	quickly	qk^y
pursue	prsu	quiet	qet
pursuit	prst	quietly	qet^y
push	p_s	quit	qt
put	pt	quite	qit
puzzle	pzl	quiver	qvr
		quorate	qrt
		quorum	qrm
		quota	qta
		quotation	qta^n
		quote	qot
		quotient	qtint
		Quran	qrn

qualification	$qlfc^n$ / qual
qualify	qlfy
quality	qlty
quantify	qntfy
quantity	qnty
quarantine	qrntn
quarrel	qrl
quart	qrt
quarter	1/4
quarterback	qrtrbk
quash	q_s
queen	qn
quell	ql
quench	qn_c
querying	qry^g

R

rabbit	rbt
raccoon	rcn
race	rc
racial	r^s
racism	rcsm
rack	rk
radar	rdr
radiance	rd^c
radiant	rdint
radiate	rdit
radiation	rdi^n
radical	rdcl
radio	rdo
radiography	rdogrphy / rdogrfy
radiotherapy	$rdo_t rpy$
raffle	rfl
rage	rg
raid	rd
rail	rl
railroad	rlrd
rain	rn
raise	rs
raised	rsd
rally	r^y
ramble	rmbl
ramification	$rmfc^n$
rampage	rmpg / rmpj
ran	rn
ranch	rn_c
random	rndm
randomized	rndmizd
range	rng
rank	rnk
ranked	rnkd
ransom	rnsm
rant	rnt
rape	rp
raped	rpd /rapd
rapid	rpd
rapidly	rpd^y
rapture	rptr
rare	rr
rarely	rr^y / r^y
rash	r_s
rasp	rsp
raspberry	rspbry
rat	rt
ratchet	$r_c t$
rate	rt
rather	$r_t r$
ratify	rtfy
rating	rt^g
ratio	rto
ration	rs^n
rational	r^{nl}
rationale	$r^n al$
rattle	rtl
ravage	rvg / rvj
raw	rw
razor	rzr
re	r /re
reabsorb	rabsrb
reach	r_c
react	ract
reaction	rac^n
reactive	ractv

read	rd	rebuke	rbuk
reader	rdr	recall	rcl
readership	rdr^p	recalled	rcld
readily	rd^y	recap	rcp
reading	rd^g	recapture	rcptr
readjust	rajst	recede	rced
readmission	radm^n	receipt	rcpt
readmit	radmt	receive	rcv
ready	rdy	received	rcvd
reaffirm	rafrm	receiver	rcvr
real	rl	receivership	rcvr^p
realign	raln	recent	rcnt
realignment	raln^m	recently	rcnt^y
realistic	ralstc	reception	rcp^n
reality	ralty	recess	rcs
realize	ralz	recession	rcs^n
really	r^y	recharge	r$_c$rg
realm	rlm	recipe	rcp
reappear	rapr	recipient	rcpnt
reapply	rap^y	reckon	rkn
rear	rr	reclaim	rclm
rearrange	rarng	reclamation	rclm^n
rearrest	rarst	recline	rcln
reason	rsn	recognition	rcgn^n
reasonable	rsn^b	recognize	rcgnz
reassert	rasrt	recollect	rclct
reassess	rass	recommend	rcmnd
reassign	rasin	recommendation	rcmnd^n
reassurance	rasr^c	reconcile	rcncl
reassure	rasr	reconstruct	r^{c}strct
rebalance	rbl^c	record	rcrd
rebate	rbt	recording	rcrd^g
rebel	rbl	recoup	rcop
rebound	rbnd	recover	rcvr
rebuff	rbf	recovery	rcv^y
rebuild	rbld	recreate	rcret

recreating	rcret^g	reflection	rflc^n
recreation	rcre^n	reflex	rflx
recreational	rcre^{nl}	reflux	rflx
recruit	rcrt	refocus	rfcs
recruitment	rcrt^m	reform	rfrm
rectify	rctfy	refrain	rfrn
rector	rctr	refresh	rfr$_s$
recuperate	rcprt	refreshment	rfr$_s{}^m$
recur	rcr	refrigerator	rfrgrtr /frg/frj
recurrence	rcr^c	refuel	rful
recycle	rcycl	refuge	rfg / rfj
red	rd	refugee	rfge / rfje
redact	rdct	refund	rfnd
redeem	rdem	refurbish	rfrb$_s$
redefine	rdfn	refurbishment	rfrb$_s{}^m$
redeploy	rdply	refuse	rfs
redeploying	rdply^g	regain	rgn
redirect	rdrct	regard	rgrd
redouble	rdbl	regarding	rgrd^g
redraft	rdrft	regardless	rgrdls
redress	rdrs	regime	rgm
reduce	rdc	regiment	rg^m
reduction	rdc^n	region	rgn / rjn
redundant	rdndnt / rdnt	regional	rgnl
re-emergence	remrg^c	register	rgstr
reenact	renact	registrar	rgstrr
reenaction	renac^n	regrade	rgrad
re-evaluate	revlut	regress	rgrs
refer	rfr	regression	rgr^n
referee	rfre	regret	rgrt
reference	rfr^c	regroup	rgrp
referred	rfrd	regular	rglr
refinance	rfn^c	regularly	rglr^y
refine	rfn	regulate	rglt
refit	rft	regulated	rgltd
reflect	rflct	regulation	rgl^n

regulator	rgltr	relegate	rlgt
regulatory	rglt^y	relegation	rlg^n
rehabilitation	rhblt^n	relent	rlnt
rehearsal	rhrsl	relevance	rlv^c
rehearse	rhrs	relevant	rlvnt
rehome	rhm	reliability	rli^{bty}
rehomed	rhmd	reliable	rli^b
rehouse	rhs	reliance	rli^c
rehydrate	rhydrt	relief	rlf
rehydration	rhydr^n	relieve	rlv
reimburse	rimbrs	religion	rlgn
reindeer	rndr	religious	rlgos
reinfection	rinfct^n	relish	rl$_s$
reinforce	rinfrc	relocate	rlct
reinstate	rinstt	relocation	rlc^n
reinvent	rinvnt	reluctant	rlctnt
reinvest	rinvst	rely	r^y
reiterate	ritrat	remain	rmn
reject	rjct	remaining	rmn^g
rejection	rjct^n	remark	rmrk
rejoice	rjc	remarkable	rmrk^b
rekindle	rkndl	rematch	rmt$_c$
relabel	rlbl	remedial	rmdil
relapse	rlps	remedy	rmdy
relate	rlt	remember	rmbr / rem
related	rltd	remembrance	rmbr^c
relation	rl^n	remind	rmnd
relationship	rla^{np}	reminded	rmndd
relative	rltv	reminder	rmndr
relatively	rltv^y	remission	rm^n
relativity	rltvty	remittance	rmt^c
relaunch	rln$_c$	remorseful	rmrs^f
relax	rlx	remote	rmt
relaxation	rlx^n	removal	rmvl
relaxing	rlx^g	remove	rmv
release	rles	renal	rnl

render	rndr	representative	$r^{p}sntv$ / rep
renounce	rnn^{c}	repress	$r^{p}s$
renovate	rnvt	repression	r^{pn}
renovation	rnv^{n}	reprieve	rprv
renown	rnwn	reprint	rprnt
rent	rnt	reproachful	$r^{p}{}_{c}{}^{f}$
rental	rntl	reproduce	$r^{p}dc$
renumbering	$rnmbr^{g}$	republic	rpblc
reoccupy	rocpy	Republican	rpblcn
reopen	ropn	repulsive	rplsv
reoperate	roprt	reputable	rpt^{b}
reorder	rordr	reputation	rpt^{n}
repackage	rpkg / rpkj	request	rqst
repair	rpr	require	rqr
reparation	rpr^{n}	required	rqrd
repay	rpy	requirement	rqr^{m}
repayment	rpy^{m}	rescue	rscu
repeat	rpt	research	rsr_{c}
repeated	rptd	researcher	$rsr_{c}r$
repeatedly	$rptd^{y}$	reselect	rslct
repel	rpl	resell	rsl
repetition	rpt^{n}	reseller	rslr
replace	rplc	resemble	rsmbl
replaceable	$rplc^{b}$	resentful	$rsnt^{f}$
replacement	$rplc^{m}$	reservation	$rsrv^{n}$
replay	rply	reserve	rsrv
replicate	rplct	reshuffle	$r_{s}{}^{f}$
replies	rpls	residence	$rsdn^{c}$
reply	rp^{y}	resident	rsdnt
report	rprt	residential	$rsdn^{s}$
reported	rprtd	resign	rsn
reportedly	$rprtd^{y}$	resignation	$rsgn^{n}$
reporter	rprtr	resilience	rsl^{c}
reporting	$rprt^{g}$	resilient	rslnt
represent	$r^{p}snt$	resist	rsst
representation	$r^{p}snt^{n}$		

resistance	rsst^c	resuscitation	rsct^n
resolution	rsl^n	retail	rtl
resolve	rslv	retailer	rtlr
resolved	rslvd	retain	rtn
resonance	rsn^c	retaliate	rtlit
resort	rsrt	retard	rtrd
resound	rsnd	retch	r$_c$
resource	rsrc	retention	rnt^n
resourceful	rsrc^f	rethink	r$_t$nk
respect	rspct	retire	rtr
respectable	rspct^b	retired	rtrd
respectful	rspct^f	retirement	rtr^m
respectfully	rspct^{fy}	retouch	rt$_c$
respectively	rspctv^y	retract	rtrct
respiration	rspr^n	retractable	rtrct^b
respiratory	rsprt^y	retraction	rtrc^n
respond	rspnd	retrain	rtrn
respondent	rspndnt	retreat	rtrt
response	rsp^c	retribution	rtrb^n
responsibility	rspn^{bty}	retrieve	rtrv
responsible	rspn^b	retrospect	rtrspct
responsibly	rspn^{by}	retrospective	rtrspctv
rest	rst	retrospectively	rtrspctv^y
restaurant	rstrnt	return	rtrn
restful	rst^f	reunite	runt
restoration	rstr^n	reusable	rus^b
restore	rstr	reuse	rus
restrain	rstrn	revamp	rvmp
restrict	rstrct	reveal	rvl
restriction	rstrc^n	revelation	rvl^n
restroom	rstrm	revenge	rvng / rvnj
result	rslt	revenue	rvnu
resume	rsm	reverence	rvr^c
resurface	rsrfc	reverse	rvrs
resurgence	rsrg^c	reversible	rvrs^b
resuscitate	rsctt	reversing	rvrs^g

revert	rvrt	ring	r^g
review	rwv	ringfence	r^{g}f^c
reviewed	rvwd	riot	riot
revise	rvis	rip	rp
revision	rv^n	rise	rs
revisit	rvst	risen	rsn
revive	rvv	risk	rsk
revoke	rvk	risky	rsky
revolution	rvlu^n	ritual	rtl
revolutionary	rvlu^{ny}	rival	rvl
revolve	rvlv	river	rvr
revulsion	rvl^n	road	rd
rewaken	rawkn	roadholding	rdhld^g
reward	rwrd	roadmap	rdmp
reword	rwrd	roam	rm
rewritten	rrtn	rob	rb
rhetoric	rtrc	robbed	rbd
rhinoceros	rnocrs	robber	rbr
rhyme	rym	robin	rbn
rhyming	rym^g	robot	rbt
rhythm	r$_t$m	rock	rk
rib	rb	rocket	rkt
ribbon	rbn	rod	rd
rice	rc	role	rl / rol
rich	r$_c$	roll	rl
rid	rd	rolling	rl^g
ride	rd / rid	Roman	rmn
rider	rdr	romance	rm^c
ridge	rg / rj	romantic	rmntc
ridicule	rdcul	roof	rf
ridiculous	rdculos	room	rm
riding	rd^g	root	rt
rifle	r^f	rope	rp
right	rt	rose	rs
rightful	rt^f	rotate	rtt
rim	rm	rotation	rt^n

rough	rf
roughly	rf^y
round	rnd
route	rt /rot
routine	rtn
routinely	rtn^y
row	rw
royal	ryl
rub	rb
rubber	rbr
ruin	run
rule	rl
ruling	rl^g
rumble	rmbl
rumor	rmr
run	rn
runner	rnr
running	rn^g
rupture	rptur
rural	rrl
rush	r$_s$
Russian	rs^n
rust	rst

S

sabotage	sbtg / sbtj
sack	sk
sacred	scrd
sacrifice	scrfc
sad	sd
sadly	sd^y
safe	sf
safekeeping	sfkp^g
safely	sf^y
safety	sfty
said	sd
sail	sl
sake	sk
salad	sld
salary	sl^y
sale	sl / sal
sales	sls
salient	slint
saliva	slva
salmon	smn / slmn
salt	slt
salute	slut
salvage	slvg / slvj
same	sm
sample	smpl
sampling	smpl^g
sanction	snc^n
sand	snd
sandwich	sndw$_c$
sanitized	sntzd
sat	st
satellite	stlt

satisfaction	stsfc^{n}	school	scl
satisfactory	stsfct^{y} / sat	science	si^{c}
satisfy	stsfy	scientific	sintfc
saturate	strt	scientist	sintst
saturation	stra^{n}	scold	scld
Saturday	sa	scope	scp
sauce	sc	scorch	scr$_{c}$
savage	svg / svj	score	scr
save	sv	scorn	scrn
saver	svr	Scotland	sctlnd / sct
saving	sv^{g}	scramble	scrmbl
savor	svr	scrap	scrp
savory	sv^{y}	scrape	scrap
savvy	svy	scratch	scr$_{c}$
saw	sw	scream	scrm
say	sy / sa	screen	scrn
saying	sy^{g}	screening	scrn^{g}
scald	scld	screw	scrw
scale	scl	scribble	scrbl
scan	scn	scribe	scrb
scandal	scndl	script	scrpt
scandalize	scndliz	scrub	scrb
scanner	scnr	scrutinize	scrtnz
scar	scr	scuffle	scfl
scare	scr /scar	sculpt	sclpt
scared	scrd	sculpture	sclptr
scary	sc^{y}	sea	c
scatter	sctr	seahorse	chrs
scavenge	scvng / scvnj	seal	sl
scenario	scnro	search	sr$_{c}$
scene	scn	season	ssn
scent	snt	seat	st
schedule	scdl	seclusion	scl^{n}
scheme	scm	second	scnd / 2nd
scholar	sclr	secondary	scnd^{y} / 2nd^{y}
scholarship	sclr^{p}	seconded	scndd / 2ndd

Word	Abbrev.	Word	Abbrev.
seconder	scndr / 2ndr	semblance	smbl^c
secondment	scnd^m / 2nd^m	semi-detached	smi-dt$_c$d
seconds	2nd / secs	seminar	smnr
secret	scrt	Senate	snt /snat
secretary	scrt^y	senator	sntr
section	sc^n	send	snd
sectioned	sc^{n}d	senior	snr
sector	sctr	sensation	sns^n
secular	sclr	sensational	sns^{nl}
secure	scr	sense	s^c
securely	scr^y	sensitive	snstv
security	scrty	sensitivity	snstvty
sedate	sdt	sent	snt
sediment	sd^m	sentence	snt^c
seduction	sdc^n	sentencing	snt^{cg}
see	c	sentiment	snt^m
seed	sd / cd	separate	sprt
seeing	c^g	separation	spr^n
seek	sk	September	se
seem	sm	sequence	sq^c
seemingly	sm^{gy}	sequential	sqn^s
seethe	s$_t$	sergeant	srgnt
segment	sg^m	serialize	srialz
segregate	sgrgt	series	srs
segregation	sgrg^n	serious	sros
seize	sz	seriously	sros^y
seizure	szr	servant	srvnt
seldom	sldm	serve	srv
select	slct	service	srvc
selected	slctd	serving	srv^g
selection	slc^n	session	s^n
self	slf	set	st
self-esteem	slf-estm	setback	stbk
selfish	slf$_s$	setting	st^g
sell	sl	settle	stl
seller	slr	settlement	stl^m

settling	stl^y	sheath	$_st$
seven	7	shed	$_sd$
seventeen	17	sheep	$_sp$
seventh	7th / 7_t	sheer	$_sr$
seventy	70	sheet	$_st$
sever	svr	shelf	$_slf$
several	svrl	shell	$_sl$
severance	svr^c	shelter	$_sltr$
severe	svr	shelve	$_slv$
severely	svr^y	shelving	$_slv^g$
sex	sx	shepherd	$_sprd$
sexual	sxul / sxl	sheriff	$_srf$
sexuality	sxulty / sxlty	shield	$_sld$
sexually	sx^y	shift	$_sft$
sexy	sxy	shine	$_sn$ / $_sin$
shade	$_sd$	shingles	$_sngls$
shaded	$_sdd$	ship	^{p} / $_sp$
shades	$_sds$	shipment	^{pm} / $_sp^m$
shadow	$_sdw$	shipping	^{pg} / $_sp^g$
shake	$_sk$	shirk	$_srk$
shall	$_sl$	shirt	$_srt$
shallow	$_slw$	shit	$_st$
shambles	$_smbls$	shiver	$_svr$
shame	$_sm$	shock	$_sk$
shameful	$_sm^f$	shoe	$_so$
shape	$_sp$	shoestring	$_sostr^g$
share	$_sr$	shoot	$_st$ / $_sot$
shared	$_srd$	shooting	$_st^g$ / $_sot^g$
shareholder	$_srhldr$	shop	$_sp$
shark	$_srk$	shoplift	$_splft$
sharp	$_srp$	shopper	$_spr$
sharpen	$_srpn$	shopping	$_sp^g$
sharply	$_srp^y$	shore	$_sr$
shave	$_sv$	short	$_srt$
she	sh / s	shortage	$_srtj$ / $_srtg$
sheaf	$_sf$		

shortbread	$_s$rtbrd	sift	sft
shortcoming	$_s$rtcm^g	sigh	sgh / si
shorten	$_s$rtn	sight	st
shortfall	$_s$rtfl	sign	sn
shortly	$_s$rt^y	signage	sng / snj
shorts	$_s$rts	signal	sgnl
short-term	$_s$rt-trm	signature	sgntr / sig
shot	$_s$t	significance	sgnf^c
should	$_s$d	significant	sgnfcnt
shoulder	$_s$ldr	significantly	sgnfcnt^y
shout	$_s$t	signify	sngfy
shove	$_s$v	signpost	snpst
shovel	$_s$vl	Sikh	sk /skh
show	$_s$w / $_s$o	silence	sl^c
showcasing	$_s$wcs^g	silent	slnt
shower	$_s$wr	silk	slk
shred	$_s$rd	silly	s^y
shrewd	$_s$rwd	silver	slvr
shrimp	$_s$rp	similar	smlr
shrink	$_s$nk	similarity	smlrty
shrivel	$_s$rvl	similarly	smlr^y
shrug	$_s$tg	simmer	smr
shudder	$_s$dr	simple	smpl
shuffle	$_s$fl	simplify	smplfy
shut	$_s$t	simply	smp^y
shutter	$_s$tr	simulate	smult
shuttle	$_s$tl	simultaneously	smltnos^y/ sim
shy	$_s$y	sin	sn
sibling	sbl^g	since	s^c
sick	sk	sinful	sn^f
sicken	skn	sing	s^g
side	sd	singer	s^{g}r
sideline	sdln	single	s^{g}l
sidewalk	sdwlk	sink	snk
siege	sg / sj	sir	sr
		sister	sstr / sis

sit	st	slide	sld /slid
site	st / sit	slight	slt
situation	stua^n	slightly	slt^y
six	6	slimline	slmln
sixteen	16	sling	sl^g
sixth	6th / 6$_t$	slip	slp
sixty	60	slippage	slpg / slpj
size	sz	slither	sl$_t$r
skeleton	skltn	slogan	slogn
ski	ski	slope	slop
skid	skd	slot	slt
skill	skl	sloth	sl$_t$
skilled	skld	slow	slw / slo
skillful	skl^f	slowly	slw^y /slo^y
skim	skm	slug	slg
skin	skn	sluggish	slg$_s$
skip	skp	sluice	slc
skirt	skrt	slumber	slmbr
skulking	sklk^g	slump	slmp
skull	skl	slur	slr
skunk	sknk	smack	smk
sky	sky	small	sml
slack	slk	smart	smrt
slacken	slkn	smash	sm$_s$
slam	slm	smattering	smtr^g
slander	slndr	smell	sml
slant	slnt	smile	sml / smil
slap	slp	smiling	smil^g
slash	sl$_s$	smirk	smrk
slave	slv	smoke	smk
slavery	slv^y	smoking	smk^g
sleep	slp	smolder	smldr
sleeve	slv	smooth	sm$_t$
slender	slndr	smother	sm$_t$r
slice	slc	smuggle	smgl
slick	slk	snack	snk

snail	snl	soldier	sldier / sljr
snake	snk /snak	sole	sl
snap	snp	solely	sl^y
snatch	sn$_c$	solicitor	slctr
sneak	snk	solid	sld
sneakers	snks	solution	sl^n
sneaky	snky	solve	slv
sneer	snr	solving	slv^g
sneeze	snz	some	sm
snivel	snvl	somebody	smbdy
snore	snr	someday	smdy
snow	sno	somehow	smhw
so	so	someone	smon / sm1
soak	sk	something	sm$_t$^{g}
soar	sr	sometime	smtm
sob	sb	sometimes	smtms
sober	sbr	somewhat	sm$_w$t
so-called	so-cld	somewhere	sm$_w$r
soccer	scr	son	sn
social	s^s / so^s	song	sng
socialized	s^{s}lzd	soon	sn / son
socializing	s^{s}lz^g	sophisticated	sfstctd
socially	s^{sy}	sorry	s^y
society	scty	sort	srt
sock	sk	soul	sl /sol
socket	skt	sound	snd
sodium	sdm / na	soup	sp / sop
sofa	sfa	source	src
soft	sft	south	s$_t$ / s
soften	sfn	southeast	se
softly	sft^y	southern	s$_t$rn
software	sftwr	southwest	sw
soil	sol	sovereignty	svrnty
solar	slr	Soviet	svt
sold	sld	sow	sw
solder	sldr	space	spc

spaniel	spnl	spiritual	sprtl
Spanish	spn$_s$	spit	spt
spare	spr	spite	spit
spark	sprk	spiteful	spt^f
sparrow	sprw / spro	splash	spl$_s$
spatial	sp^s	splint	splnt
speak	spk	split	splt
speaker	spkr	spoke	spk
spec	spc	spokesman	spksmn
special	sp^s	spokesperson	spksprsn
specialist	spst	spokeswoman	spkswmn
specialize	sp^{sz}	sponsor	spnsr
specialty	sp^{sty}	sponsorship	spnsr^p
species	spcs	spoon	spn / spon
specific	spcfc	sport	sprt
specifically	spcfc^y	sporty	sprty
specify	spcfy	spot	spt
spectacular	spctclr	spouse	sps /spos
spectra	spctra	spray	spry
spectroscopy	spctrscpy	spread	sprd
spectrum	spctrm	spring	spr^g
speculate	spclt	sprinkle	sprnkl
speculation	spcl^n	sprint	sprnt
speech	sp$_c$	spy	spy
speed	spd	squad	sqd
spell	spl	squander	sqndr
spend	spnd	square	sqr / □
spending	spnd^g	squash	sq$_s$
sphere	sfr	squeeze	sqz
spill	spl	squint	sqnt
spin	spn	squirm	sqrm
spinal	spnl	squirrel	sqrl
spine	spn / spin	stability	st^{bty}
spinster	spnstr	stabilize	st^{b}z
spiral	sprl	stable	st^b
spirit	sprt	stack	stk

stadium	stdm /stad	stay	sty
staff	stf	steadily	std^y
stage	stg / stj	steady	stdy
stagger	stgr	steak	stk / stek
staggering	stgr^g	steal	stl / stel
stagnate	stgnat	steam	stm
stair	str	steel	stl / stel
stairway	strwy	steep	stp / step
stake	stk	steer	str /ster
stalemate	stlmt	stem	stm
stance	st^c	step	stp
stand	stnd	stereotype	strotp
standard	stndrd	sterile	stril
standing	stnd^g	sterilize	strliz
staple	stpl	steroid	stroid
star	str	steward	stwrd
stare	str / star	stick	stk
start	strt	stiff	stf
starter	strtr	still	stl
starting	strt^g	stimulate	stmlt
startle	strtl	stimulus	stmls
starvation	strv^n	sting	st^g
starve	strv	stink	stnk
state	stt	stipulate	stpult
stated	sttd	stipulation	stpul^n
statement	stt^m	stir	str
static	sttc	stitch	st$_c$
station	st^n	stock	stk
stationary	st^{ny}	stocking	stk^g
stationery	st^{ny}	stockpile	stkpl
statistic	sttstc / stat	stocktake	stktk
statistical	sttstcl	stomach	stm$_c$
statistics	sttstcs / stats	stone	stn
statue	sttu	stood	std
status	stts	stop	stp
statute	sttt	storage	strg /strj

store	str	struggle	strgl
storm	strm	student	stdnt
story	st^y	studio	stdo
stove	stv	study	stdy
straight	strt	stuff	stf
straighten	strtn	stumble	stmbl
strain	strn /stran	stupid	stpd
strange	strng	stutter	sttr
stranger	stngr	style	styl
strangle	strgnl	stylish	styl$_s$
strapline	strpln	sub adolescence	^{s}adls^c
strategic	strtgc	sub adult	^{s}adlt
strategy	strtgy	subatomic	^{s}atmc
straw	strw	subcategory	^{s}ctg^y
strawberry	strwbry	subcommittee	^{sc}te
streak	strk	subconscious	^{sc}sos
stream	strm	subconsciousness	^{sc}sosns
street	strt / st	subcontinent	^{sc}tnnt
strength	strng$_t$	subcontract	^{sc}trct
strengthen	strng$_t$n	subcontractor	^{sc}trctr
stress	strs	subculture	^{s}cltr
stretch	str$_c$	subdivide	^{s}dvd
strict	strct	subdivision	^{s}dv^n
strictly	strct^y	subdue	^{s}du
strife	strf	subeditor	^{s}edtr
strike	strk	subgroup	^{s}grp
striking	strk^g	subheading	^{s}hd^g
string	str^g	subject	^{s}jct
stringent	strngnt	subjective	^{s}tjctv
strip	strp	sublease	^{s}les
strive	strv	sublet	^{s}lt
stroke	strk	sublevel	^{s}lvl
strong	strng	sublimate	^{s}lmt
strongly	strng^y	sublime	^{s}blim
structural	strctrl	subliminal	^{s}lmnl
structure	strctr	submerge	^{s}mrg

submission	^{s}m^n	subtly	st^y
submissive	^{s}tmsv	subtotal	^{s}ttl
submit	^{s}mt	subtract	^{s}trct / -
subnormal	^{s}nrml	subtraction	^{s}trc^n / -^{n}
subnormality	^{s}nrmlty	subtropical	^{s}trpcl
subordinate	^{s}ordnt	suburb	^{s}urb
subpoena	^{s}pena	suburban	^{s}urbn
subscribe	^{s}scrb	suburbia	^{s}rba
subscript	^{s}scrpt	subversion	^{s}vr^n
subsect	^{s}sct	subversive	^{s}vrsrv
subsequent	^{s}sqnt	subway	^{s}wy / ^{s}wa
subservient	^{s}srvint	succeed	scd
subset	^{s}st	success	scs
subside	^{s}sid	successful	scs^f
subsidence	^{s}sd^c	successfully	scs^{fy}
subsidiary	^{s}sdi^y	succession	scs^n
subsidize	^{s}sdiz	such	s$_c$
subsidy	^{s}sdy	suck	sk
subsistence	^{s}sst^c	suction	sc^n
subsoil	^{s}sl	sudden	sdn
substance	^{s}stn^c	suddenly	sdn^y
substandard	^{s}stndrd	sue	su
substantial	^{s}stn^s	suffer	sfr
substantially	^{s}stn^{sy}	suffering	sfr^g
substantiate	^{s}stntt	sufficient	sfcnt
substantive	^{s}stntv	suffix	sfx
substation	^{s}st^n	suffocate	sfct
substitute	^{s}sttut	suffocation	sfc^n
substitution	^{s}stt^n	sugar	sgr
subsume	^{s}sum	suggest	sgst
subtext	^{s}txt	suggested	sgstd
subtitle	^{s}ttl	suggestion	sgs^n
subtitled	^{s}ttld	suicide	suicd
subtitles	^{s}ttls	suit	st
subtle	stl	suitable	st^b / sut^b
subtlety	stlty	suite	sut

sum	sm	supernormal	^{s}nrml
summarize	smriz	supernumerary	^{s}nm^y
summary	sm^y	superpose	^{s}imps
summer	smr	superscript	^{s}scrpt
summit	smt	supersede	^{s}cd
summon	smn	superseded	^{s}cdd
sun	sn	supersensitive	^{s}snstv
Sunday	su	superset	^{s}st
sundry	snd^y	supersize	^{s}sz
sunlight	snlt	superstar	^{s}str
sunny	sny	superstition	^{s}st^n
super	^{s}	superstitious	^{s}stsos
superannuated	^{s}anutd	superstore	^{s}str
superb	^{s}b	supervise	^{s}vs
superbly	^{s}b^y	supervision	^{s}v^n
supercharger	^s_crgr	supervisor	^{s}vsr
supercilious	^{s}clios	supervisory	^{s}vs^y
superficial	^{s}f^s	supper	^{s}r
superficially	^{s}f^{s}y	supple	^{s}l
superfine	^{s}fn	supplement	^{s}l^m
superfluous	^{s}fluos	suppleness	^{s}lns
superglue	^{s}glu	supplicant	^{s}lcnt
superheavyweight	^{s}hvywt	supplied	^{s}ld
superhero	^{s}hro	supplier	^{s}lir
superheroine	^{s}hroin	supply	^{s}y
superhighway	^{s}hwy	support	^{s}rt
superhuman	^{s}hmn	supporter	^{s}rtr
superimpose	^{s}imps	supportive	^{s}rtv
superintelligent	^{s}intlgnt	suppose	^{s}ps
superintendent	^{s}intndnt	supposed	^{s}psd
superior	^{s}ir	supposedly	^{s}psd^y
superiority	^{s}irty	supposition	^{s}ps^n
superlative	^{s}ltv	suppress	^{s}prs
supermarket	^{s}mkt	suppression	^{s}pr^n
supermodel	^{s}mdl	supremacy	^{s}rmcy
supernatural	^{s}ntrl	supreme	^{s}rem

surcharge	$sr_c r^g$	suture	sutr
surcharging	$sr_c rg^g$	swab	swb
sure	sr / $_s r$	swallow	swlw
surely	sr^y	swear	swr
surface	srfc	sweat	swt
surfeit	srft	sweater	swtr
surfing	srf^g	sweep	swp /swep
surgeon	srgen	sweet	swt /swet
surgery	srg^y	swell	swl
surgical	srgcl	swerve	swrv
surmountable	$srmnt^b$	swim	swm
surname	srnm	swimming	swm^g
surpass	srps	swindle	swndl
surplus	srpls	swing	sw^g
surprise	srprs	switch	sw_c
surprised	srprsd	sword	swrd
surprising	$srprs^g$	sycamore	scmr
surprisingly	$srprs^{gy}$	syllable	sl^b
surrogate	srgt	symbol	smbl
surround	srnd	symbolic	smblc
surrounding	$srnd^g$	symbolize	smbliz
surveillance	$srvl^c$	sympathy	$smp_t y$
survey	srvy	symptom	smptm
surveyor	srvyr	syndicate	sndct
survival	srvvl	syndrome	sndrm
survive	srvv	syringe	srng / srnj
survivor	srvvr	system	sstm
susceptible	$sspt^b$		
suspect	sspct		
suspend	sspnd		
suspension	$sspn^n$		
suspicion	ssp^n		
suspicious	sspcos		
sustain	sstn		
sustainable	$sstn^b$		
sustenance	$sstn^c$		

T

table	t^b
tabled	t^bd
tablespoon	t^bspn / tbs
taboo	tbo
tabulated	tbultd /tab
tack	tk
tackle	tkl
tactful	tct^f
tactic	tctc
tactical	tctcl
tadpole	tdpl
tag	tg
tagged	tgd
tail	tl
tailgating	$tlgt^g$
tailor	tlr
take	tk
taken	tkn
taking	tk^g
tale	tl / tal
talent	tlnt
talented	tlntd
talk	tlk
tall	tl
tangible	tng^b
tangle	tngl
tank	tnk
tantalize	tntlz
tantalizing	$tntlz^g$
tap	tp
tape	tp / tap
taper	tpr
target	trgt
tariff	trf
tarnish	trn_s
task	tsk
taste	tst
tasteful	tst^f
taunt	tnt
tax	tx
taxable	tx^b
taxation	tx^n
taxi	txi
taxpayer	txpyr
tea	t /te
teach	t_c
teacher	t_cr
teaching	t_c^g
team	tm
teammate	tmmt
tear	tr
tearful	tr^f
tease	ts
teaspoon	tspn
technical	t_cncl
technician	t_cn^n
technique	t_cnq
technological	t_c^{ol}
technology	t_c^o
teen	tn /ten
teenage	tng /tnj
teenager	tngr / tnjr
teetering	ttr^g
teeth	t_t
teetotal	tettl
telecasting	$tlecst^g$

teleconference	tl^{c}fr^c	terrible	tr^b
telephone	tlephn / tlefn / tel	terribly	tr^{by}
telescope	tlscp	terrific	trfc
television	tlv^n / tv	terrify	trfy
tell	tl	territory	trt^y
temper	tmpr	terror	trr
temperament	tmpr^m	terrorism	trrsm
temperamental	tmpr^{ml}	terrorist	trrst
temperature	tmprtr/ temp	terrorize	trrz
template	tmplt	tertiary	trt^y
temple	tmpl	test	tst
temporary	tmpr^y	testament	tst^m
tempt	tmpt	testify	tstfy
temptation	tmpt^n	testimony	tstmny
tempted	tmptd	testing	tst^g
ten	10	testosterone	tststrn
tenancy	t^{c}y	tether	t$_t$r
tenant	tnnt	text	txt
tend	tnd	textbook	txtbk
tendency	tnd^{cy}	textile	txtl
tender	tndr	texture	txtr
tendon	tndn	than	$_t$n / tn
tennis	tns	thank	$_t$nk
tense	t^c	thank you	tx / $_t$x / $_t$nk u
tension	tn^n	thankful	$_t$nk^f
tent	tnt	thankfully	$_t$nk^{fy}
tentative	tnttv	thanking	$_t$nk^g
tenth	10th / 10$_t$	thanks	$_t$x / $_t$nks
term	trm	Thanksgiving	$_t$xgv^g/$_t$nksgv^g
terminal	trmnl	that	$_t$t / tht
terminate	trmnt	that is	ie
termination	trmn^n	thatch	$_t$c
terms	trms	thaw	$_t$w
terrace	trc	the	$_t$ / th / . / 7
terrain	trn /tran	theater	$_t$tr

Word	Shorthand	Word	Shorthand
their	$_t$r / thr	thoroughly	$_t$rgh^y
them	$_t$m / thm	those	$_t$os / thos
theme	$_t$em	though	$_t$o
themself	$_t$mslf	thought	$_t$t
themselves	$_t$mslvs	thoughtful	$_t$t^f
then	$_t$n / thn	thoughtfully	$_t$t^{fy}
theological	$_t$ol	thousand	1000
theology	$_t$o	thread	$_t$rd
theoretical	$_t$rtcl	threat	$_t$rt
theory	$_t$y	threaten	$_t$rtn
therapist	$_t$rpst	three	3
therapy	$_t$rpy	threshold	$_t$rshld
there	$_t$r / thr	thrift	$_t$rft
thereby	$_t$rby / thrby	thrive	$_t$rv
therefore	∴	throat	$_t$rt
thermal	$_t$rml	thrombosis	$_t$rmbss
these	$_t$s / ths	throttle	$_t$rtl
they	$_t$y / thy	through	$_t$ru
thick	$_t$k	throughout	$_t$ruot
thicken	$_t$kn	throw	$_t$rw
thief	$_t$f	thrust	$_t$rst
thieving	$_t$v^g	Thursday	th
thigh	$_t$i	thus	$_t$s
thin	$_t$n	thwarted	$_t$wrtd
thing	$_t$g	thyroid	$_t$rod
think	$_t$nk	tick	tk
think tank	$_t$nktnk	ticket	tkt
thinking	$_t$nk^g	tickle	tkl
third	3rd / 1/3	tide	td
thirst	$_t$rst	tidy	tdy
thirteen	13	tie	ti
thirty	30	tier	tr / ter
this	$_t$i / thi	tiger	tgr
thorax	$_t$rx	tight	tt
thorn	$_t$rn	tighten	ttn
thorough	$_t$rgh	tightly	tt^y

tile	tl /til	ton	tn
till	tl	tone	tn / ton
tilt	tlt	tongue	tng
timber	tmbr	tonight	2nt
time	tm	too	2
time saver	tmsvr	took	tk
time saving	tmsv^g	tool	tl
timekeeping	tmkp^g	tooth	t$_t$
timetable	tmt^b	top	tp
timing	tm^g	topic	tpc
tingle	tngl	Torah	trh
tinker	tnkr	torment	tr^m
tinted	tntd	torrential	trn^s
tiny	tny	tortoise	trts /trtos
tip	tp	torture	trtr
tire	tr	toss	ts
tired	trd	total	ttl
tissue	tsu	totaling	ttl^g
titillating	ttlt^g	totally	tt^y
title	ttl	totter	ttr
to	2	touch	t$_c$
toad	td /tod	touchdown	t$_c$dn / t$_c$dwn
toast	tst	tough	tgh / tf
tobacco	tbco	tour	tr
today	2dy	touring	tr^g
toddler	tdlr	tourism	trsm
toe	to	tourist	trst
together	tg$_t$r / 2g$_t$r	tournament	trn^m
toilet	tlt	tow	tw
token	tkn	toward	twrd /2wrd
told	tld	towards	twrds /2wrds
tolerance	tlr^c	towel	twl
tolerate	tlrt	tower	twr
toll	tl	town	tn / twn
tomato	tmto	toxic	txc
tomorrow	tmro / tom	toy	ty

trace	trc / trs	transformation	$t$frma^n
track	trk	transfusion	$t$fu^n
traction	trc^n	transgender	$t$gdr
trade	trd	transience	ti^c
trading	trd^g	transient	$t$ient
tradition	trd^n	transistor	$t$istr
traditional	trd^{nl}	transit	tt
traditionally	trd^{ny}	transition	ti^n
traffic	trfc	translate	$t$lt
tragedy	trgdy	translated	$t$ltd
tragic	trgc	translation	tl^n
trail	trl	translator	$t$ltr
trailer	trlr	transmission	tm^n
train	trn	transmit	$t$mt
trainer	trnr	transmitter	$t$mtr
training	trn^g	transparency	tp^{cy}
trait	trt	transparent	$t$prnt
trajectory	trjct^y	transpire	$t$pr
trample	trmpl	transplant	$t$plnt
trance	tr^c	transplantation	$t$plnta^n
tranche	trn$_c$	transport	$t$prt
transact	$t$act	transportation	$t$prta^n
transaction	$t$act^n	transpose	$t$ps
transactional	$t$act^{nl}	transposed	$t$psd
transcend	tnd	transposes	$t$pss
transcontinental	$t$ctnntl	transposition	$t$ps^n
transcribe	$t$crb	transsexual	$t$sxual / t
transcript	$t$crpt	transverse	$t$vrs
transcription	$t$crp^n	transvestite	$t$vstit
transfer	$t$fr	trap	trp
transferable	$t$fr^b	trash	tr$_s$
transfigure	$t$fgr	trashing	tr$_s$^{g}
transfigured	$t$fgrd	trauma	trma
transfix	$t$fx	travel	trvl
transfixed	$t$fxd	traveler	trvlr
transform	$t$frm		

traverse	trvrs	truly	tr^y
trawling	trwl^g	trumpet	trmpt
tray	try	truncate	trnct
treasure	trsr	truncated	trnctd
treat	trt	trunk	trnk
treatment	trt^m	trust	trst
treaty	trty	trustee	trste
treble	trbl / x3	trusteeship	trste^p
tree	tre	truth	tr_t
trek	trk	truthful	tr_t^f
tremble	trmbl	try	t^y
tremendous	trmndos	T-shirt	$t\text{-}_s rt$
trench	trn_c	tube	tub
trend	trnd	tuck	tk
trepidation	trpd^n	Tuesday	tu
trespass	trsps	tuft	tft
triage	trig / trij	tug	tg
trial	trl /tril	tuition	tui^n
triangle	trngl / Δ	tumble	tmbl
tribal	trbl	tumor	tmr
tribe	trb	tune	tun
tribulation	trbul^n	tunnel	tnl
trick	trk	turbulence	trbl^c
trigger	trgr	turbulent	trblnt
trim	trm	turf	trf
trip	trp	turkey	trky
triumph	trmf	turn	trn
troop	trp	turnover	trnovr
trophy	trphy / trfy	turtle	trtl
tropical	trpcl	tutor	ttr
trouble	trbl	tutorial	ttrl
troubled	trbld	TV	tv
truant	trunt	tweak	twk
truck	trk	tweet	twt
trudge	trg / trj	twelfth	12th / 12_t
true	tru	twelve	12

twentieth	20th /20_t
twenty	20
twice	twc / x2
twin	twn
twinned	twnd
twist	twst
twitching	tw_c^g
twitter	twtr
two	2
two-thirds	2/3
type	typ
typecasting	$typcst^g$
typesetting	$typst^g$
typewriting	$typrt^g$
typical	tpcl
typically	tpc^y
typing	typ^g
tyranny	tyrny

U

ugly	ug^y
uh	uh
ulcer	ulcr
ulceration	$ulcr^n$
ultimate	ultmt
ultimately	$ultmt^y$
ultimatum	ultmtm/ ultm
ultrasound	ultrsnd
umpire	umpr
unable	un^b
unappealing	$unapel^g$
unavailable	$unavl^b$
unavoidable	$unavd^b$
unbearable	$unbr^b$
unbeatable	$unbt^b$
unbreakable	$unbrk^b$
uncaring	$uncr^g$
uncertain	uncrtn
uncertainty	uncrtnty
unchanging	$un_c ng^g$
uncle	uncl
uncomfortable	$un^c 4t^b$
uncouth	unc_t
uncover	uncvr
undecided	undcdd
undemanding	$undmnd^g$
undeniable	$undni^b$
under	u
underachieve	$^u a_c v$
underachievement	$^u a_c v^m$
underactive	$^u actv$

underactivity	^{u}actvty	underpowered	^{u}pwrd
underarm	^{u}arm	underprepared	^{u}pprd
underbelly	^{u}b^y	underpriced	^{u}pricd
underbid	^{u}bd	underprivileged	^{u}prvlgd
undercarriage	^{u}crg / ^{u}crj	underrate	^{u}rt
undercharge	^u_cg	underrated	^{u}rtd
underclass	^{u}cls	underreported	^{u}rprtd
underclothes	^{u}cl$_t$s	underscore	^{u}scr
undercoat	^{u}ct	underscored	^{u}scrd
undercut	^{u}ct	undersell	^{u}sl
underdeveloped	^{u}dvlpd / ^{u}dev	underside	^{u}sd
underdog	^{u}dg	undersize	^{u}sz
undereducated	^{u}edctd	understaffed	^{u}stfd
underemployed	^{u}emplyd	understand	^{u}stnd
underestimate	^{u}estmt	understandable	^{u}stnd^b
underestimation	^{u}estm^n	understandably	^{u}stnd^{by}
underexpose	^{u}xps	understanding	^{u}stnd^g
underfed	^{u}fd	understate	^{u}stt
undergo	^{u}go	understated	^{u}sttd
undergoing	^{u}g^g	understatement	^{u}stt^m
undergraduate	^{u}grdut/ ^{u}grd	understood	^{u}std
underground	^{u}grnd	understrength	^{u}strng$_t$
undergrowth	^{u}grw$_t$	understudy	^{u}stdy
underhand	^{u}hnd	undertake	^{u}tk
underinvestment	^{u}invst^m	undertaken	^{u}tkn
underlay	^{u}ly	undertaker	^{u}tkr
underline	^{u}ln	undertone	^{u}tn
underlined	^{u}lnd	undertook	^{u}tk
underlying	^{u}ly^g	underused	^{u}usd
undermine	^{u}mn	underutilize	^{u}tlz
underneath	^{u}n$_t$	undervaluation	^{u}vlu^n
underpaid	^{u}pd	undervalue	^{u}vlu
underpay	^{u}py / ^{u}pa	underwater	^{u}wtr
underpayment	^{u}p^m	underway	^{u}wy
underpin	^{u}pn	underweight	^{u}wt
underpinned	^{u}pnd	underwent	^{u}wnt

underwrite	^{u}rt	universal	unvrsl
underwritten	^{u}rtn	universe	unvrs
undeserving	un^{d}rv^g	university	unvsty / uni
undesirable	un^{d}r^b	unknowing	unnw^g
undisclosed	un^{d}clsd	unknown	unnwn
undoing	und^g	unlawful	unlw^f
uneasy	unesy	unleash	unl$_s$
uneconomic	uneco	unless	unls
uneducated	unedctd	unlikable	unlk^b
unemployed	unempld	unlike	unlk
unemployment	unempl^m	unlikely	unlk^y
unenviable	unenv^b	unload	unld
unethical	une$_t$cl	unlock	unlk
uneventful	unevnt^f	unmanageable	unmnj^b /
unexpected	unxpctd		unmng^b
unfair	unfr	unnerve	unnrv
unfaithful	unf$_t$^{f}	unofficial	unof^s
unfavorable	unfvr^b	unopposed	unopsd
unfold	unfld	unpack	unpck
unfortunately	un^{f}tnt^y /	unprecedented	un^{p}cdntd
	un4tnt^y	unprintable	unprnt^b
ungrateful	ungrt^f	unreachable	unr$_c$^{b}
unhappy	unhpy	unreadable	unrd^b
unhelpful	unhlp^f	unreasonable	unrsn^b
unification	unifc^n	unreliable	unrl^b
uniform	unfrm	unsettling	unstl^g
uninsurable	uninsr^b	unsociable	unsc^b
unintentionally	unintn^{ny}	unsocial	uns^s
union	unn	unspeakable	unspk^b
unique	unq	unstable	unst^b
unit	unt	unstoppable	unstp^b
unite	unt /unit	unsuitable	unst^b
United	untd /utd	untenable	untn^b
uniting	unt^g	unthinkable	un$_t$nk^b
unity	unty		

unthinking	$un_t nk^g$	utility	utlty
untidy	untdy	utilize	utilz
until	untl	utterance	utr^c
untouchable	$unt_c{}^b$		
untraceable	$untrc^b$		
unusable	$unus^b$		
unusual	unusl		
unutterable	$unutr^b$		
unwavering	$unwvr^g$		
unwitting	$unwt^g$		
unworkable	$unwrk^b$		
up	up		
upcoming	$upcm^g$		
update	updt		
upgrade	upgrd		
uplifting	$uplft^g$		
upmarket	upmrkt		
upon	upn		
upper	upr		
uprising	$uprs^g$		
upset	upst		
upshot	$up_s t$		
upstage	upstg / upstj		
upstairs	upstrs		
urban	urbn		
urchin	$ur_c n$		
urge	urg		
us	us		
usable	us^b		
use	us		
used	usd		
useful	us^f		
user	usr		
using	us^g		
usual	usl		
usually	us^y		

V

vacancy	vcncy / vac
vacation	vc^n
vaccination	vcn^n
vaccine	vcin
vacuum	vcm
valid	vld
validate	vldt
validation	vld^n
validity	vldty
valley	vly
valuable	vlu^b / vl^b
valuation	vlu^n
value	vlu
van	vn
vanish	vn_s
vaporize	vprz
variable	vri^b
variance	vri^c
variation	vri^n
variety	vrty
various	vros
varnish	vrn_s
vary	v^y
vascular	vsclr
vast	vst
vegetable	vgt^b / veg
vegetation	vgt^n
vehicle	vhcl
vending	vnd^g
vendor	vndr
venerable	vnr^b
vengeance	vng^c
ventilate	vntlt
ventilation	$vntl^n$
venture	vntr
verb	vrb
verbal	vrbl
verbatim	vrbtm
verdict	vrdct
verge	vrg / vrj
verging	vrg^g
verifiable	$vrfi^b$
verified	vrfd
verify	vrf
verse	vrs
version	vs^n
versus	vrss /vs
vertebra	vrtba
vertical	vrtcl
very	v
vessel	vsl
veteran	vtrn
veto	vto
via	va
viable	vi^b
vibrant	vbrnt
vibrate	vbrt
vibration	vbr^n
vicar	vcr
victim	vctm
victimize	vctmiz
victorious	victros
victory	vct^y
video	vdo
video conference	vdo $^cfr^c$
view	vw
viewer	vwr

vigilance	vgl^c	vowel	vwl
vigilant	vglnt	voyage	vyg / vyj
village	vlj / vlg	vs	vs
violate	vlt	vulgar	vlgr
violation	vl^n	vulnerable	vlnr^b
violence	vl^c		
violent	vlnt		
viral	vrl		
virtual	vrtl		
virtually	vrt^y		
virtue	vrtu		
virus	vrs		
visible	vs^b		
vision	v^n		
visit	vst		
visitor	vstr		
visual	vsl /visul		
vital	vtl		
vivisection	vvsc^n		
vocabulary	vcbl^y / vocab / vcb		
vocal	vcl		
vocalize	vcliz		
vocals	vcls		
vocation	vc^n		
voice	vc		
void	vd		
volume	vlm /vol		
voluntary	vlnt^y		
volunteer	vlntr		
vomit	vmt		
vote	vt		
voter	vtr		
voting	vt^g		
vouch	v$_c$		
voucher	v$_c$r		

wage	wj / wg
waged	wjd / wgd
wagon	wgn
waist	wst
wait	wt
wake	wk
Wales	wls
walk	wlk
walking	wlk^g
wall	wl
wander	wndr /wandr
want	wnt
war	wr
warehouse	wrhs
warm	wrm
warmth	wrm$_t$
warn	wrn
warning	wrn^g
warpath	wrp$_t$
warrant	wrnt
warranty	wrnty
warrior	wrr
warship	wr^p
was	ws
wash	w$_s$
wasp	wsp
wastage	wstj / wstg
waste	wst
wasteful	wst^f
watch	w$_c$
watchdog	w$_c$dg

watchful	w$_c$^{f}
water	wtr / h2o
wave	wv
way	wy
we	w
weak	wk
weaken	wkn
weakness	wkns
wealth	wl$_t$
wealthy	wl$_t$y
weapon	wpn
wear	wr
wearable	wr^b
weather	w$_t$r
weave	wv /wev
web	wb
webcast	wbcst
wedding	wd^g
Wednesday	we
weed	wd
week	wk
weekday	wkdy
weekend	wknd
weekly	wk^y
weigh	wgh
weight	wt
weird	wrd
welcome	wlcm
welfare	wlfr
well	wl
well-being	wl-b
well-known	w-nwn
went	wnt
were	wr
west	wst / w
western	wstrn

wet	wt
whale	$_w{}^l$
what	wh / $_w$
whatever	$_w$evr
wheat	$_w{}^t$
wheel	$_w{}^l$ / $_w$el
wheelchair	$_w{}^l{}_c{}^r$
when	whn / $_w$n
whenever	$_w$nevr
where	whr / $_w{}^r$
whereas	$_w$ras
wherever	$_w$revr
whether	wt^r
which	$_{wc}$
while	whl / $_w$l
whip	$_w$p
whisky	$_w$sky
whisper	$_w$spr
whistle	$_w$stl
white	$_w{}^t$
who	$_w{}^o$
whoever	$_w$oevr
whole	$_w{}^l$
wholesale	$_w$lsl
whom	$_w$m
whose	$_w{}^s$
why	y
wide	wd
widely	wd^y
widespread	wdsprd
widow	wdo
width	wd$_t$
wield	wld
wife	wf
wild	wld
wilderness	wldrns
wildlife	wldlf
will	wl
willing	wl^g
willingness	wl^{g}ns
win	wn
winch	wn$_c$
wind	wnd
window	wndo
windpipe	wndpp
wine	wn /win
wing	w^g
winner	wnr
winter	wntr
wipe	wp
wire	wr
wireless	wrls
wisdom	wsdm
wise	ws
wish	$w_s{}^f$
wishful	$w_s{}^f$
wistful	wst^f
with	wi / w$_t$
withdraw	w$_t$drw
withdrawal	w$_t$drwl
withhold	w$_t$hld
within	w/i w/ n
without	w/o w/ou
witness	wtns
wives	wvs
wolf	wlf
woman	wmn
women	wmn / wmen
won't	wnt

wonder	wndr		
wonderful	wndr^f		
wood	wd		
wooden	wdn		
word	wrd		
work	wrk		
workable	wrk^b		
worker	wrkr		
workforce	wrkfrc		
working	wrk^g		
workmanship	wrkmn^p		
workout	wrkot		
workplace	wrkplc		
works	wrks		
workshop	wrk$_s$p		
workstation	wrkst^n		
world	wrld		
worldwide	wrldwd		
worried	wrd		
worry	w^y		
worse	wrs		
worsen	wrsn		
worship	wr^p		
worth	wr$_t$		
would	wd		
wound	wnd		
wow	wo		
wrap	wrp / rp		
wrist	wrst /rst		
write	rt		
writer	rtr		
writing	rt^g		
written	rtn		
wrong	rng		
wrong doing	rngd^g		
wrote	wrt / wrot		

XYZ

x-rated	xrtd
x-ray	xry
yard	yrd
yeah	yh
year	yr
yell	yl
yellow	ylw
yes	ys / y / ✔
yesterday	ystrdy
yet	yt
yield	yld
you	u
young	yng
youngster	yngstr
your	ur
yours	urs
yourself	urslf
youth	y$_t$
youthful	y$_t$^{f}
youthfully	y$_t$^{fy}
zeal	zl
zebra	zbr
zen	zn
zenith	zn$_t$
zone	zn
zoo	zo
zoological	z^{o}cl
zoology	z^o

**Speed Writing
Modern Shorthand
An Easy to Learn
Note Taking System**

**Heather Baker
ISBN: 978-1532704918**

Learn a new hand writing system in a matter of hours and become really quick in just a few weeks.

* This book is laid out in easy to follow lessons
* Practical guided exercises, with example answers
* Save time and become efficient at taking dictation, in meetings, on the telephone and in lectures
* No strange squiggles to learn – just different ways to use the letters you already know
* Your notes will be easy to read and transcribe
* Adapt the system to suit your needs

A terrific opportunity to save time and become more efficient.

"I am thoroughly enjoying learning a new skill from a book that is so simple to understand and I have already started to implement it."

"I will use this system all the time."

"This is so easy to learn and use."

Made in the USA
Monee, IL
07 January 2024

51342004R00075